Diarmuid Gavin

OUTER SPACES

Diarmuid Gavin

OUTER
SPACES

70

112

154

198

238

To John Noel Linnen—a good man

CONTENTS

LONDON, NEW YORK, MUNICH, MELBOURNE, DELHI

Published in the United States by DK Publishing, Inc., 375 Hudson Street, New York, New York 10014

03 04 05 06 07 10 9 8 7 6 5 4 3 2 1
ISBN 0-7894-9635-6

Discover more at www.dk.com

I come from a safe, loving, suburban background in Dublin, Ireland.

Safe, because it seemed to me that nothing exciting ever happened in

my home village of Rathfarnham. Once, not so long ago, the trams

terminated here, and walkers setting off into the Dublin mountains

were a familiar sight. Now it is one of the gateways to

suburban existence—row upon row of leafy streets lined

with semi-detached houses, all with a front and back

garden. Facilities are good and we have great parks,

woodlands, shops, and schools. We even have a castle.

I've lived in Dublin for 35 years, and during that time I've

seen many changes, but it remains a compact, friendly city,

with beautiful seaside and rolling hills within a half an hour

of wherever you are. You get used to the climate, which is

maritime—a lack of extremes of hot or cold, and lots of

rain and gray skies—but on a clear, sunny day

there's no better place on earth.

As a child and adolescent I was an introverted

dreamer, not particularly good at school—it didn't

seem to mean anything to me. I was an outdoor

person, always in trouble for leading friends astray

in Huckleberry Finn–style adventures. I loved the

natural landscape, and I developed an awareness of design. I was intrigued by both city and

countryside, and from early on, I knew I wanted to make gardens. The prototype plot was,

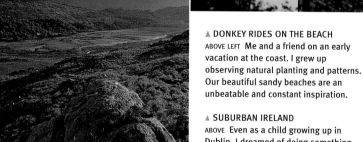

▲ FUTURISTIC DESIGN
ABOVE I often feel like I'm on a great adventure, with new concepts to explore, new materials to work with. Inspiration is all around; you just have to open your eyes, be receptive. I'm lucky that my clients are willing to journey with me.

▲ DONKEY RIDES ON THE BEACH
ABOVE LEFT Me and a friend on an early vacation at the coast. I grew up observing natural planting and patterns. Our beautiful sandy beaches are an unbeatable and constant inspiration.

▲ SUBURBAN IRELAND
ABOVE Even as a child growing up in Dublin, I dreamed of doing something exciting with those monotonous rows of dreary front and back yards.

◄ COUNTY KERRY
LEFT Wild, open expanses, breathtaking mountain scenery... when I'm away from home, I can just close my eyes and conjure up the emerald-green grass, the gray stone covered with yellow lichen, soft purple heathers, and hazy cloud-strewn skies. My country's natural beauty is my most valuable resource.

of course, my parents' garden, and my career has probably been the result of a reaction against conformity and prettiness. I always knew I wanted to do something different, but I didn't know how.

After school I worked in a plant shop in the city center for three years and learned the basics. Then I studied at the College of Amenity Horticulture, National Botanic Gardens, Glasnevin from 1985 to 1988. These were probably my most formative years, and I had great fun. I learned a lot about plants and an awful lot about life, but very little about design. At the time I thought I'd missed out but, in retrospect, it meant I had to formulate my own ideas and decide where I wanted to go, and what I wanted to do. This wasn't easy. Suggesting or trying anything different was met with derision by the gardening establishment. Pretty gardens were the order of the day. Collecting and growing plants was what everybody aspired to. Design was frowned upon, especially anything new. I could design pretty gardens without a problem; I could win awards, but it just left me frustrated.

The solution came when I built a garden at the Chelsea Flower Show in 1996. It was a vibrant, city garden that made

▲ VILLAGE OF SNEEM
ABOVE Perhaps it's a knee-jerk reaction to the gray clouds that so often blanket our country, but we Irish have a great love of color. The main street in Sneem, County Kerry, is a kaleidoscope, with each house painted a different shade—the effect is, literally, brilliant.

▲ THE NATURAL BEAUTY OF IRELAND
ABOVE RIGHT I'm often bowled over by the sheer beauty around me in local parks and gardens. In terms of perfect planting, what designer could improve on this lily-filled pond?

▲ BOTANICAL GARDENS, GLASNEVIN
ABOVE The greenhouse at the National Botanic Gardens at Glasnevin, on the outskirts of Dublin, is very familiar territory. I spent many hours here between classes while studying at the College of Amenity Horticulture.

▶ DUBLIN CITY CENTER
RIGHT My home city is now one of Europe's most vibrant cultural centers. Great memories, great *craic*! I love it here.

▶ CONCRETE DUCKS
RIGHT A humorous detail from a garden in Leitrim, central Ireland. Three concrete ducks bobbing in a natural stream are the essence of fun.

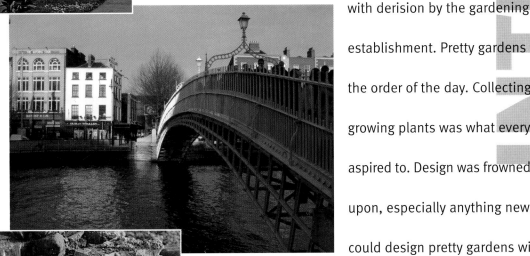

the most of new technology and materials that people weren't used to seeing outside. Exotic plants, glass water walls, and slabs in the lawn that lit up at night— all these combined to create a garden with a nightclub feel. It wasn't done particularly well, I now realize, and it was ignored as far as prizes went, but it did lead to a career in designing and creating gardens for television. The BBC became a patron, and I'm grateful to them for introducing me to clients and picking up most of the bill for the contemporary gardens I was now free to create.

As a result, I've had a fantastic and dynamic seven years, working with inspiring collaborators and having many of my designs brought to life. I've learned a huge amount, and I've had a chance to push forward the boundaries of garden design and explore the possibilities of every site. The gardens are varied. Whether they are good or bad, who knows? Certainly, I have made mistakes, but with every project I've undertaken, I've tried to do my very best.

It's been great fun, though, and I hope you enjoy some of the fruits of an ongoing venture.

◄ THREE-TIERED GARDEN
LEFT I love building gardens for shows, not for the glory of winning, but because they allow me the freedom to create something new, something for me. This garden, shown at the Royal Dublin Society Garden Festival in 1996, was on three levels, with a sun terrace at the top, a dining area (shown here) just below it, and a garden with a pool at ground level. It was at this time that I started to experiment with modern materials, which have become central to my current work.

▲ TRADITIONAL TO MODERN
ABOVE In 1995 I was still building fairly conventional gardens like this one, which was exhibited at the Royal Dublin Society show. It later became the garden for a local pub.

◄ COMMISSIONED PIECE
LEFT I had my own landscape and design business in Dublin for a few years after I graduated. This garden was designed for a private client who wanted a sun terrace overlooking a colorful flower garden. The dining table is built from railroad ties.

▲ SPACESHIPS AND WILD WATERS

ABOVE AND ABOVE RIGHT The garden above, designed in 1996 for the Royal Hospital Kilmainham Garden Festival, is one of the first gardens to include a spaceship—an idea that has now become something of a trademark. The design on the right is my first Chelsea show garden, which I called "To the waters and the wild" after W.B. Yeats' poem "The Stolen Child."

▶ URBAN COOL

RIGHT (TWO PICTURES) As an unknown designer, I needed publicity for my urban city garden at the 1996 Chelsea Flower Show. Philip Treacy, the award-winning Irish hat designer, kindly sent along his muse, wearing one of his most outrageous creations, to be photographed with me. The press took a few shots and I did a short televised interview with Alan Titchmarsh.

▼ TELEVISION SUCCESSES

BELOW (THREE PICTURES) Amazingly, my brief chat with Alan at Chelsea led to a television series that allowed me to create the gardens I'd always dreamed of. Below is a garden from an early program; the middle shot is of a glass brick tunnel linking a communal garden to a parking lot; and the design on the right is one of my favorites, affectionately known as "Curvy."

PHILOSOPHIES

The joy of gardening, a love of plants, and passion for good design and exciting architecture are the elements that drive me to create beautiful gardens

HEROES

I don't come from a gardening background, and Mum and Dad's gardening skills involved keeping things neat, and introducing color with bedding plants and alpines. I always hated this. So, although my parents are my heroes, for garden inspiration I look elsewhere: to television, books, and to other people's designs.

I love creative people who are generous with their time, and this applies to the gardeners I admire. I'll start with Helen Dillon because she's from home—in fact, for a few years we lived on the same street—and because her achievements at Ranelagh, an elegant, formal town garden in Dublin, are sublime. She also writes passionately and beautifully.

John Brookes, Russell Page, and Sylvia Crowe form a group of mentors whose books explaining the evolution of a new style I have devoured. I also love the work of Tony Heywood and Ivan Hicks, who have demonstrated with great panache that it's possible to be gardeners *and* passionate about developing surreal ideas within a landscape. Beth Chatto explores the potential of every site and situation, and I am in awe of the wonderful plants she grows at her nursery in Colchester, England. And Dr. David Hessayon—whose *Expert* series of books is underrated by many in my profession—is worthy of respect for bringing gardening to a huge number of people.

Alan Titchmarsh, too, has opened up the whole world of gardening to everyone in a delightful and sensible way without any pretensions.

And finally, for analyzing the potential of the future, and for showing me exciting, innovative gardens around the world, there's no work to match that of Guy Cooper and Gordon Taylor.

▶ JOHN BROOKES
RIGHT When I was studying, John Brookes was the person who excited me most. His books on small gardens were the first to show me that something new and viable was happening.

▶ TONY HEYWOOD'S SURREALISM
CENTER Tony Heywood is one of a number of surreal gardeners I admire. He has an exceptional outlook, and a magical ability to realize his visions and build gardens of extraordinary quality.

▶ RUSSELL PAGE'S INFLUENCES
FAR RIGHT If there's just one book you should read, it's *The Education of a Gardener* by Russell Page, a man who truly understood his craft.

▶ HELEN DILLON
RIGHT Ireland's most important gardener, Helen Dillon is a plantswoman like no other. Her garden in Ranelagh, Dublin, is one of the best town gardens anywhere.

▶ ALAN TITCHMARSH
CENTER Almost single-handedly, Alan Titchmarsh has brought gardening to a new audience. His practical approach and sensible outlook have deservedly made him the foremost British gardener.

▶ SYLVIA CROWE
FAR RIGHT A brilliant innovator, Sylvia Crowe had an inherent knowledge of combining materials, textures, and planting to create incredible public and private spaces.

▶ DR. HESSAYON
RIGHT Dr. David Hessayon is one of the world's best-selling authors. He writes very simple books on basic gardening in a clear and concise way.

▶ BETH CHATTO
CENTER Beth Chatto explores the diversity of situations in our gardens, and has shown how—working in various conditions and environments—to make the most of different sites.

▶ IVAN HICKS'S INSPIRATIONS
FAR RIGHT This man is a free spirit whose gardens inspire children, senior citizens, and everyone in between, but he is often dismissed as too quirky.

◀ GUY COOPER AND GORDON TAYLOR
LEFT Known as the curious gardeners, this pair appears regularly on the BBC. They are passionate about gardens, wherever they might be in the world.

HEROES

Apart from the natural landscape, nothing exists on its own. Gardens aren't isolated from other creative forms, and gardeners see, use, and feel many different things during the day.

I've always been interested in art and design, and I'm fascinated by the process of how things are made and created—whether by traditional skills or by contemporary technology. I love to feel and touch different materials, and to explore their potential. It's the combination of watching what other people do, examining the excitement they create, the tools they use, and the ideas they put forward that leads me to attempt to cross-pollinate the world of horticulture with that of architecture, fashion and furniture design, art, and video.

The people who inspire me from these various circles are those who challenge perception, working with line, shape, form, and function to create something that defies expectation. Some are contemporaries, but they also include visionaries whose work in the first half of the 20th century has been hugely influential. When looking at classic pieces of architecture and design from this period, it's easy to forget how brave and ground-breaking the designers were for their time. People like Le Corbusier, Luis Barragán, Roberto Burle Marx, Arne Jacobsen, Eileen Gray, and Frank Lloyd Wright defied every convention, and I'm still being informed by

▲ ARNE JACOBSEN
TOP There were three main categories of architect Arne Jacobsen's forms: waves and lines, natural, and geometric. His buildings were often criticized, but his Egg chair (shown here) was a worldwide sensation.

▲ ROBIN AND LUCIEN DAY
ABOVE Husband and wife Robin and Lucien Day created furniture (including some TVs) and textiles, respectively. I always find inspiration in their ground-breaking work.

◄ PHILIP TREACY
LEFT Philip Treacy's hats are fantastic. I love the fact that he's totally unbound by convention; his designs look more like sculptures.

their work today. I'm also learning from contemporary artists: the creative, challenging works of milliner Philip Treacy, fashion designer Alexander McQueen, architect Zaha Hadid, and design practitioners Future Systems are exhilarating and push me to take my designs further. Their bravery is an inspiration to us all.

◄ FUTURE SYSTEMS
LEFT Built in 1994, this is Future Systems' Hauer-King House in London. Made of glass, it uses the nearby trees to provide shade and privacy. It also blends inside and out: the same tiles are used on the interior floor as in the back garden.

▼ FRANK LLOYD WRIGHT
BELOW Frank Lloyd Wright believed that American architecture should develop "in the image of trees." How could I disagree? The New York Guggenheim is one of his most famous and brilliant pieces of architecture.

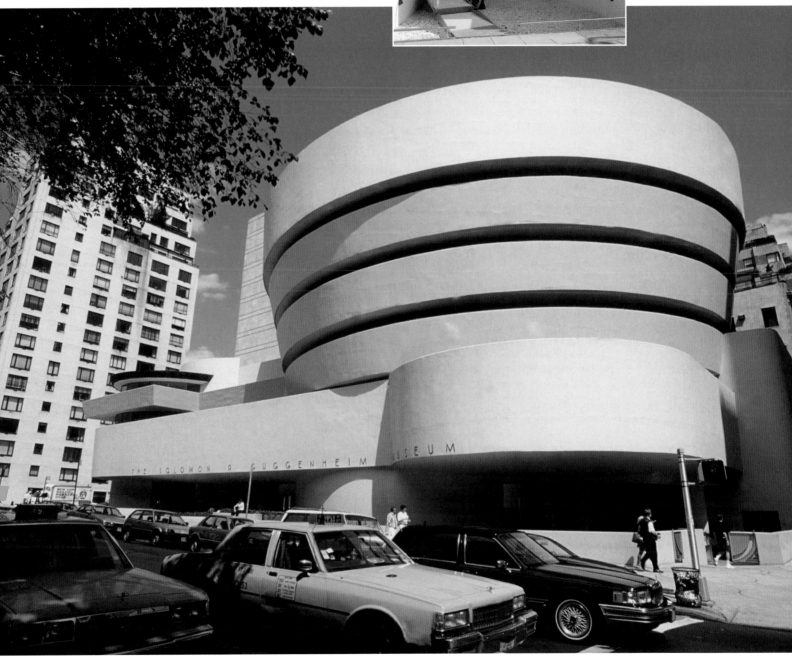

MODERNISM

Modernism is the name given to a specific style developed in the 1930s by architects such as Michael Scott in Ireland, Le Corbusier in France, Ludwig Mies van der Rohe in Germany, and Luis Barragán in Mexico. Although a few Modernists designed outdoor spaces, the style generally passed gardens by. Until today, that is, when many designers have usurped the movement's title and poorly mimicked its smooth, sleek lines to produce gardens that are starkly architectural, ordered, precise, and, to my mind, soulless. And soulless is exactly what Modernism was not. When Luis Barragán built his famous stables at San Cristobal, he bravely and passionately pushed the boundaries to create a vibrancy and excitement that I believe all gardens should have.

Contemporary gardens should reflect the way we live now, not life in the 1930s, and use the materials and technology at our disposal today. It's just plain lazy to reproduce, rather than try to surpass, a style that was new and exciting 70 years ago.

The same goes for some Western designers' obsession with Zen gardens. In Japan, such gardens have deeply spiritual, philosophical, and social meaning; they fulfill a purpose and are an integral part of the Japanese lifestyle. They also reflect the fact that land in Japan is limited and that gardens, like the houses and towns they are a part of, have to be squeezed into small spaces between the mountains and the sea. Transported to the West, such gardens become pure ornamentation. Deprived of their original meaning and context, the shapes within them,

▲ PRIZES BUT NO PASSION
ABOVE This garden by Christopher Bradley-Hole —which won a gold at the 2000 Chelsea Flower Show in London—increased awareness of a modern approach to garden design but, to me, it lacks passion.

► PURE ZEN
RIGHT This Zen garden in a London square was created for the Hempel Hotel and has always struck me as the antithesis of where we should be today in terms of design. Its formulaic layout shows little originality, and I would not describe it as contemporary.

▼ CREATING FOCUS
BELOW The symmetry, clean lines, and beautiful execution of this Chelsea show garden create a sense of order that people crave, but it reflects a Modernist style that was developed over 70 years ago, and I think it says nothing about how we live today.

which are profoundly important in Japan, merely pretend to have significance here and look unconvincing.

That's not to say there aren't contemporary garden designers doing great work with tremendous passion. People like Mary Reynolds and the designers of Parc André Citroën in Paris, for example, refuse to conform to what's become accepted as the "modern" style: Reynolds' work is old-fashioned in some ways, yet it shows a passion for the natural world; and Parc André Citroën is truly modern, and reflects the lifestyle of the people who use it. If we are to create meaningful contemporary gardens, the idioms we employ have to be as heartfelt as these examples—not bad copies of a tried-and-tested style that makes them look more like anonymous living rooms.

To me, modern gardens are contemporary gardens—and most contemporary gardens display an absolute misunderstanding of what the word means—that is, influenced by what's happening today. We can't continue to just include all the perceived ingredients of Modernity and expect the results to work as outside spaces. We need to reassess our attitudes, and, as garden designers, push forward and explore every ounce of creativity.

◄ MARY REYNOLDS
OPPOSITE PAGE Mary Reynolds, a young Irish designer, created *A Celtic Sanctuary Garden* for the Chelsea Flower Show in 2002. She won a gold medal, an honor that was entirely deserved. Her design captured a beauty, simplicity, and magic from another place and era, and her natural planting style reflects the mood of our time.

▲ TRADITIONAL COTTAGE GARDEN
ABOVE Gertrude Jekyll's planting style was revolutionary in its day. I love it because it shows a real appreciation of plants and how they can be combined to create fabulous pictures.

▼ PARC ANDRE CITROEN
BELOW This fantastic, modern park is a testament to the value Parisians place on their public spaces.

GARDENING

The joys to be had from gardening are immense, and they're not exclusive to any one set of people: we can all be involved. I don't like garden snobs who try to dictate the styles we choose and the plants we plant. Gardening means different things to different people.

My favorite type of gardening is digging. I dig to find out what the soil's like, what it's rich in, or what it's missing. I dig to prepare the soil, and to invest in the future of whatever I think is right to plant in it. I especially love to dig in the middle of winter when there's been a frost overnight and the ground is a little bit hard. I don't like machines to do the work for me; I want to feel the soil falling through my bare hands. I like to take out as many stones and weeds as possible, to add well-rotted manure or leaf mold where it's needed, to rake the surface and take away any debris, knowing that the job has been done well. I especially love digging with an old radio beside me, my thoughts drifting around the garden, planning, thinking about what I'm going to plant here or there, while getting snatches of conversation or song from someone else's world.

Gardening is vast and varied, and there's a tendency to want to master all of its aspects, or to feel guilty if you don't. I'm not very good on fruit trees or vegetable growing, but I look forward to having the time and the space to cultivate pumpkins and

▲ GREAT ACHIEVEMENTS
ABOVE It's a great feeling to be shown around other people's gardens, and to share their pride in their achievements.

► ALL EMBRACING
OPPOSITE PAGE (NINE PICTURES) Every gardener will tell you that they first got the bug when they were a child. At a young age, children are entranced by plants, insects, and enjoyment. They are also open to anything. We can teach them, but we can also learn from them.

▼ GETTING INVOLVED
BELOW When I visit shows, such as Chelsea, I never cease to be amazed by people's passion and enthusiasm for the gardens and plants.

GARDENING

squash, cherries and grapes, and different types of potatoes and tomatoes. I know people who mainly eat food they've grown themselves, and what an enormous source of satisfaction it is to them. They know exactly what's been put on their crops, and every day they have the pleasure of wandering out into their gardens to see what's ready for picking—or whether the pests have gotten there first.

I love so many things about gardening. My joy is setting out a garden, planting it up, and watching how the plants grow; it's in preparing an area for a herbaceous bed, understanding what the plants need to thrive; it's in looking at a shady place under a tree and trying to find something that will grow there with so little light; and it's in getting climbers established in seemingly inhospitable situations.

Two years ago I got my first garden, my own place where I could do whatever I wanted, where I could grow the plants I loved. It was a confusing site and a bit nerve-racking initially— how did I want to set it out, what did I want to grow? I became the client. As usual, all the answers presented themselves within a couple of months, and now I'm the proud curator of a lovely garden full of flowers. I walk through it every morning before I go to work to see what's coming out.

▼ THE GARDENERS' CLUB
BELOW Gardeners are exceptionally lucky people. We are united by a common interest, and so get to join one of the biggest clubs in the world. There is always something for us to read, something to watch, something to share, and there is always a fascination either with the plants themselves or with how other people have managed to cultivate and use them.

▲ IN TOUCH WITH THE SOIL
ABOVE I love being in touch with the soil, whether it's digging or weeding; I don't even mind the seemingly endless job of pulling out bindweed and couch grass. The feel of earth crumbling through my fingers is almost unbeatable.

The seasons take on a whole new meaning for gardeners. Spring is amazing: it's as if nature has this rush of blood to the head—everything wants to get going and outperform its neighbor. It's like an unstoppable party to which everyone's been invited.

▲ **KEEPING THINGS REAL**
ABOVE I'm a big fan of do-it-yourself gardening, and think it's a great idea to have your own compost pile, and to dig and weed by hand, rather than using machines or weed killers which can do more harm than good.

► ▼ **WORK, REST, AND PLAY**
RIGHT AND BELOW Working in the garden is always an absolute pleasure for me, but I can't think of a better place for rest and relaxation, either.

Summer is long and lazy, but it can be a battle to keep everything looking good, to water, and to deadhead the flowers. But it's also a time of sitting down and relaxing, of enjoying the leafy worlds we create for ourselves. Autumn, when we harvest what the plants have produced and collect up seed for next year, is also the beginning of decay, when things die away and go to ground. And winter is a time of rest and planning, when the soil collapses into inertia after a flurry of activity, and the elements do their job. But winter can be an exciting time, too, a time to look forward, to anticipate what's to come.

When you're a gardener, you're aware of life, people, the weather—and you're very aware of your surroundings because you're working so closely with nature. But don't be controlled by fashion or style. Whether you have a hanging basket bursting with bedding plants, an immaculate lawn, or a patch in a community garden, enjoy every moment.

▲ **BAMBOO**
Bamboos, like *Phyllostachys aureosulcata* f. *aureocaulis*, are great for introducing instant height into a newly planted garden.

◄ **RED-HOT POKER**
Reliable, unfussy, and fiendishly garish, red-hot pokers sizzle even on dull days. If a garden threatens to slump in late summer, I know I can always use them to inject color.

▼ **HONEY BUSH**
I love my architectural plants, and the honey bush (*Melianthus major*) is one of the best, with its beautiful blue-tinged, serrated foliage and strong shape.

Gardeners are united by their love of plants; after all, growing them is what gardening is about. As a child I was fascinated by cacti. Weird and dangerous, and inextricably linked to TV shows about cowboys and Indians, I grew them on my windowsill and collected lots of different types. I propagated them, too, and was intrigued by the fact that from one plant you could get whole families. Living stones from South Africa really got me going: they look like pebbles most of the time and then suddenly produce amazingly bright flowers from their centers.

I developed a passion for gardening through a love of the outdoors. In particular, I was fascinated by plants that have been native to Ireland's wonderful countryside for thousands of years, such as oak, ash, and hawthorn; wild flowers that light up the meadows in late spring; rustling grasses and sedges; and bog plants that flourish in the damp areas.

Trips to Cork and Kerry made me notice plants native to other countries that now grow like weeds there: dicksonias from New Zealand thrive in valleys and near the sea along the Ring of Kerry; bananas flourish in walled gardens on the islands off the coast; and brightly colored cannas, phormiums, and palms grow throughout Ireland. On visits to the amazing lunar landscape of the Burren in the west of Ireland, where alpines and trees shelter between cracks in the rock formations, I pondered the mystery of how they had arrived and adapted to such inhospitable situations.

PLANT PASSIONS

PLANT PASSIONS

I've also been lured by the thrill of the new exotics, and immersed myself in the English cottage style, as perfected by Gertrude Jekyll at her home in Munstead Wood. Jekyll worked in harmony with nature, and used herbaceous plants, introduced from around the world, to create borders awash with waves of color.

My own garden could be described as catholic, eclectic, or psychotic. I like a touch of drama. As well as cool green plants, like alchemillas, euphorbias, and hostas—all firm favorites—it also features the awesome *Melianthus major*, with its blue serrated leaves, and red-hot pokers, which are native to South Africa but grow along the cliff face in Dublin Bay, self-seeding among the sea thrift (*Armeria maritima*). Other plants include bamboo—to my mind, as at home in Irish water gardens as it is in China—and traditional cottage-style plants, such as dicentras, geraniums, foxgloves, and daylilies, which all produce amazing, exuberant flowers in soft hues and startling colors.

Growing plants will always be a journey for me. I'm already planning an all-green garden with occasional spikes of color. I can see heads of *Allium* 'Purple Sensation' exploding from clouds of clipped boxwood, and contrasting waves of *Pachysandra terminalis* and evergreen ferns. The thing about plants is that you never stop learning, and you always want to try new things.

▼ BLEEDING HEARTS
BELOW I love the beautiful heart-shaped flowers of *Dicentra spectabilis*, which explain its common name—bleeding heart. Its blooms emerge in late spring and early summer.

▼ SPURGE
BOTTOM Of the 2,000 species of spurge, my favorites are the tall architectural types, such as *Euphorbia characias*. This evergreen makes a dramatic statement in a gravel bed or mixed border throughout the year.

► HIGH AND MIGHTY
TOP ROW FROM LEFT The common foxglove (*Digitalis purpurea*) and its cultivars can reach heights of up to 6ft (2m), and each leaf of the giant *Gunnera manicata* can span 6ft (2m). Cannas are prized for their large paddle-shaped foliage, which is often variegated.

► TEXTURE AND COLOR
MIDDLE ROW FROM LEFT Textured grasses like *Stipa gigantea* often feature in my designs. The pretty, open flowers of cosmos are perfect for a cottage-style border, and tall foxtail lilies (*Eremurus robustus*) provide a vertical accent at the back of a bed.

► FLOWERS AND FOLIAGE
BOTTOM ROW FROM LEFT Daylilies, like *Hemerocallis* 'Green Flutter', have both colorful flowers and strap-like foliage. *Agapanthus* 'Snowy Owl' has beautiful white flowers, while *Hosta* 'So Sweet' has excellent variegated leaves.

Architecture and gardens are inextricably linked. Even where there are no buildings or walls in the garden, we use plants to create architectural form and shape, or as a background to more fluid planting.

Garden architecture generally falls into two categories. The first is the building attached to the site—be that a home, an office block, or even a fast-food outlet. The garden can either meld the structure with its softer surroundings, or contrast with it—making a statement by being radically different. The second type of architecture is found within the garden itself, and encompasses buildings used for storage, and rooms in which to relax and view the plants. I find most of these garden buildings bland and uninspiring: wooden boxes that don't reflect anything that's gone before in terms of architecture or what is happening now. They lack context and are best disguised with paint and plants. But this was

▲ WALES HOUSE AND BUS SHELTER
ABOVE (TWO PICTURES) Dubbed the "Teletubby House," this building designed by Future Systems looks like a spaceship that's crashed into a Welsh hillside.
    Utilitarian doesn't have to mean ugly, as this sleek, surprisingly elegant bus shelter proves.

◄ THE HEMISPHERE, EXPO 1967, MONTREAL
LEFT Strength and beauty combine in this wonderful example of a Buckminster Fuller geodesic dome.

▼ LUIS BARRAGAN'S STABLE IN SAN CRISTOBAL
BELOW This building is very theatrical, like a stage set. Bold shapes, bold colors, bold statement—I love it.

not always the case. In the past, auxiliary features in the

garden were built from the same materials as the main

property. This created an integrated look and established

a strong rule of design, which is to employ only a limited

number of materials for the hard landscaping and

structures in a garden.

My attitude to garden architecture has always been to

look beyond what's readily available, to see what you love elsewhere—

structures that inspire or excite you, make you feel fantastic or relaxed—and

then to reflect these in your own space. I think the architecture of even simple

things like bus shelters is amazing, despite their roadside setting.

Architects who inspire and excite me include Buckminster Fuller, whose

incredible geodesic domes, built in North America 50 years ago, were revolutionary; Luis Barragán,

especially in his use of stark materials and powerful colors; and Le Corbusier, who created a garden

in the sky at the Villa Savoye. The Villa is built on stilts and has a roof-terrace garden, so that views of

the landscape are framed from both inside and outside the house. The Alhambra Palace in Granada,

Spain, is another inspiration. The Moorish architecture and gardens are intertwined—you can't

imagine one without the other—and feature highly ornate courtyards, jets of water, fruit trees, and

roses, set against intricate lattice plasterwork.

My designs are architectural, but the sheds

and pavilions, paths and patios I build are

made from interesting materials and designed

to inspire—not to be hidden from view.

▲ VILLA SAVOYE
TOP Le Corbusier was a fan of reinforced concrete. A revolutionary material back in 1929, its strength allowed him to free the Villa's façade of supporting beams, enlarge the windows, and create an open-plan interior.

▲ DYMAXION HOUSE
ABOVE Buckminster Fuller's energy-efficient geodesic dome home in Wichita, KS, looks like a big top. Built in 1946, this aluminum structure has movable internal walls—inspired!

◄ RICHARD ROGERS
LEFT I'm a great fan of Richard Rogers, whose work includes the Lloyds Building in London. I particularly admire the pavilion style of this residential house, built in 1968 in south London.

THE ALHAMBRA
RIGHT This beautiful palace in Granada, Spain, makes brilliant use of the soothing, reflective qualities of water. It is a work of genius.

THE GARDENS

Places to relax, to chill out, where time stands still, just for a while. These gardens offer a space to breathe, hidden from the outside world

UNWIND

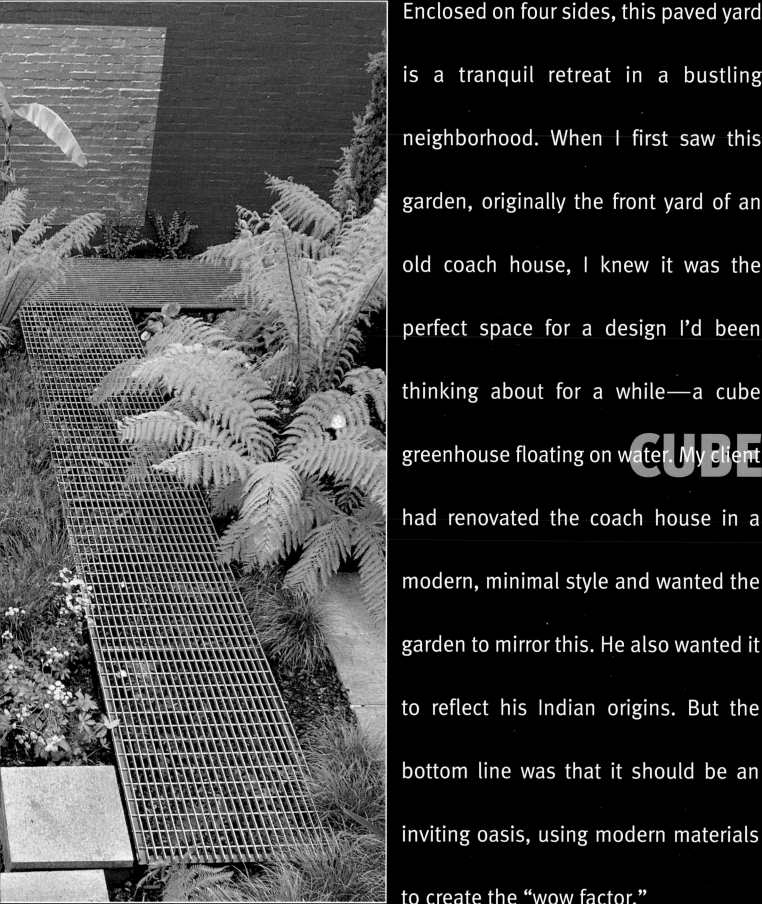

Enclosed on four sides, this paved yard is a tranquil retreat in a bustling neighborhood. When I first saw this garden, originally the front yard of an old coach house, I knew it was the perfect space for a design I'd been thinking about for a while—a cube greenhouse floating on water. My client had renovated the coach house in a modern, minimal style and wanted the garden to mirror this. He also wanted it to reflect his Indian origins. But the bottom line was that it should be an inviting oasis, using modern materials to create the "wow factor."

CUBE

INSPIRATIONS

I'd been thinking about a massive cube-shaped, glass conservatory for some time. I imagined it floating on a lake, like an ice cube in water, with an entrance via an underground tunnel, or perhaps a sort of catwalk runway. I wanted to use glass because, for me, it spells modernity: it's minimal, see-through, and it works well in both traditional and modern surroundings—the glass pyramid extension to the Louvre in Paris is a great example of this. And as well as showcasing plants, like a traditional conservatory, I thought my cube could frame a beautiful piece of furniture, creating a gallery exhibition case. It amused me to think that when you looked at it from outside with someone inside, it would frame a life, too.

The rich blue and gold walls in the garden are reminiscent of the colors used in Indian iconography, and reflect the client's Asian origins.

The thing that excited me about this garden was the nature of the site. It really was a blank canvas with loads of potential waiting to be explored. Its squareness was important, as was the fact that the walls were high. It meant that I could create anything I wanted, so long as the structure was lower than the surrounding walls.

My main idea was to create a glass building that would hover over water like a sculpture, and once this was in position on my plan, the other elements, such as the raised walkways that link other areas of the garden, just fell into place. The client wanted to use the garden for entertaining, and so I sketched in a patio along the sunniest wall, and decided to light the path leading from the house so that guests could find their way around the garden at night.

I wanted lots of color in the garden, and made the walls a brilliant blue, while the plants provide rich greens throughout. I imagined the sun reflecting off the glass cube, illuminating different parts of the garden at different times of the day, altering colors and casting dynamic shadows.

▲ ORIGINAL GARDEN
The courtyard was once an enclosed, desolate, empty space, devoid of plants and interest.

▼ SKETCHING IDEAS
The idea of using a glass cube as an outdoor room was inspired by the pyramid over the Louvre entrance in Paris and by Damien Hirst's pickled shark, with its subject framed within a glass box.

▼ FINISHED DESIGN
Tree ferns and other exotic architectural plants grow through and around the structures, blurring the hard lines with their dramatic foliage.

► MODEL GARDEN
Free of any planting, the model clearly shows the strong geometric lines of the garden's structures and paths.

I wanted as much planting as possible in this garden—I think it wa[s]
reaction against the blank paved area that hit me on my first visit t[o]
site. The plants are inspired by the client's Indian heritage, with
bananas (*Musa basjoo*), tree ferns (*Dicksonia antarctica*), umbrella
grass (*Cyperus involucratus*), cannas, and phormiums predominati[ng]
I have even planted beneath the walkways. They're made from met[al]
grilles that allow light and water to filter through to the shade-lovi[ng]
hostas, ferns, and sedges growing below them.

Flowers are present, but I have chosen those with simple, unfus[sy]
blooms, such as the beautiful white Japanese anemone 'Honorine
Jobert', and the dainty, dark red *Astrantia* 'Hadspen Blood'. Both a[lso]
have good, sculptural foliage.

FINAL PLAN
The high walls surrounding the
garden and dense planting create a
feeling of privacy and seclusion

CONCRETE CATWALK
The white concrete
walkway is inlaid with
blue glass lenses
and lit from below

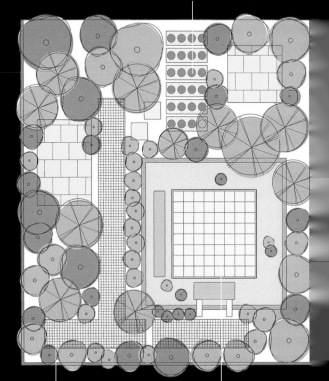

PLANTING LIST

CLOCKWISE FROM TOP LEFT
Astrantia 'Hadspen Blood'
Cyperus involucratus
Musa basjoo
Cordyline australis 'Atropurpurea'
Nymphaea 'Escarboucle'
Anemone x *hybrida* 'Honorine Jobert'
Dryopteris dilatata

METAL PATHS
Metal grilles built
above the plants
create pathways
th[rough the area]

SEE-THROUGH FLOOR
The glass cube has a
transparent floor and
stands above a
[shallow water feature]

I wanted the glass cube to be see-through from all angles—whether you were inside or looking at it from a distance—and to appear to float above a tiled pool, suspended as if hanging in midair. To achieve the right effect, it couldn't stand on a solid base or the illusion would be lost, but a stainless-steel grille offered the perfect solution. Although the cube—which has the appearance of an aquarium or a Wardian case—ended up much smaller than I had originally envisioned, I think it's still really effective.

As well as the cube, there are seating areas and walkways linking the different elements, but the main feature is the planting—the ferns and hostas that transform the garden into a magical space. I got a real sense of joy creating a garden here where none had existed. When trees are being cut down every day and delicate ecosystems destroyed, it felt fantastic to pull up paving and replace it with plants.

▲ INSIDE AND OUTSIDE THE CUBE

ABOVE (FOUR PICTURES)
The glass cube performs two different functions: it is a beautiful, simple design feature, and a place to sit and enjoy the tropical atmosphere created by the planting.

The paved area outside the cube, with its table and chairs, provides space for entertaining and offers a different perspective of the garden.

Inside the cube, the Le Corbusier recliner adds a modern note, yet is a comfortable, practical piece of furniture from which to enjoy the plants.

◄ CULTURAL INFLUENCES

LEFT This image shows how the colors and planting work together, creating an exotic garden style that reflects the client's Indian origins. The gold square painted on the far wall mirrors the shape of the cube and is a color used extensively in Indian decorative arts. Metal grille walkways are used throughout the garden to link the different features and seating areas.

► TEXTURE AND LIGHT

OPPOSITE PAGE TOP (SIX PICTURES)
Plants, such as the banana, that have a strong architectural quality complement the overall design.

The white concrete path running up to the front door is inset with blue glass lenses. Underlit at night, the blue circles create a graphic picture.

The glass cube rests on a stainless steel grille set on top of another grille made up of smaller squares. The whole structure is elevated above a tranquil pool.

► PLANTING PATTERNS

OPPOSITE PAGE BOTTOM (TWO PICTURES)
The plants inside the cube merge with those outside, allowing hardy and more tender types to sit side by side. Plants such as cordylines create a dramatic effect, their shapes casting cinematic shadows as the sun moves across the sky. Likewise, the cube changes according to the mood of the day, the amount of light,

My idea for this long, sloping garden was quite simple. Although the plot had innate charm, with majestic trees in a wooded area at the back, it needed some shape, structure, and interesting features to give it coherence. At first glance, the garden appeared too open, so I split it up into smaller spaces to create a sense of mystery and interest. The glass building evolved in response to the need for a dividing feature that was tall enough to mask the elevated land behind it. Multi-functional, it acts as a greenhouse, potting shed, and living room all in one.

GREENHOUSE

INSPIRATIONS

The simple curving line of the latest Volkswagen Beetle was the inspiration for the greenhouse, which is the architectural focal point and backdrop to the first half of the garden. Fun, yet elegant in form, it has a certain grace. I also looked at bridges with steel girders bent to form arcs. Greenhouses such as the beautiful Curvilinear Range at Glasnevin, Dublin, designed by Richard Turner, were also firmly in my mind, as were the geodesic domes at the Eden Project in Cornwall, England.

I knew that the planting would have to be simple in this garden—the clients were looking for something quite low-maintenance. But I wanted the planting to enhance the sculptural quality of the design, and while flicking through my garden books, I came across boxwood clipped into domes, which would perfectly reflect the arc of the greenhouse.

PLANS

The basis of the finished design was a building in the shape of a gentle curve that crossed the garden at an angle—to allow for extra length. The new structure was a replacement for an old greenhouse that housed seedlings and a few tomato plants. I realized that my structure would not accommodate tall tomatoes easily, which is why I designed a sunken area where the glass arc curved down.

The plot is large and I decided to cover most of it with lawn, punctuated with two raised decks set on the same diagonal as the greenhouse. Between these, I sketched in two rills, which would emerge from under the structure and planting and inject the space with sound and movement. I also wanted to enhance the wooded area behind the greenhouse, so I incorporated an arboretum, accessed through a door at the back of the greenhouse.

▶ SKETCHING IDEAS
I decided that the greenhouse should be built on a diagonal across the garden to bridge a gap between the trees and the lawn. From here, the rest of the design fell into place.

▼ SKETCHING IDEAS
A huge, arching structure, almost like a bridge, was the image I had in mind for the greenhouse.

▼ FINISHED DESIGN
The dramatic curved structure extends across the width of the garden. Its glass walls and roof convey a lightness that belies its large size.

▼ MODEL GARDEN
The sloping site meant the greenhouse had to be raised up on supports at the front. The sunken area at one end is for growing tall plants.

Planting took the form of euonymus balls clipped into cloudlike formations, and a selection of deciduous and evergreen shrubs, such as the easy-going *Aucuba japonica* and bamboolike *Nandina domestica,* grouped together along the garden boundaries.

I also planted a new arboretum behind the curved greenhouse, and used the existing mature specimens to supplement my plantings. The arboretum is filled with some of my favorite trees, including the graceful silver birch (*Betula pendula*) and the smoke bush (*Cotinus* 'Grace'), which has wonderful deep purple leaves that light up to a fiery red in autumn. I also planted a number of rowans throughout the garden, both behind and in front of the greenhouse. This tree is a particular favorite, with its wonderful divided foliage, great autumn tints, and beautiful berries.

PLANTING LIST

CLOCKWISE FROM TOP LEFT
Cotoneaster horizontalis
Euonymus fortunei 'Silver Queen'
Cotinus 'Grace'
Betula pendula
Nandina domestica
Aucuba japonica
Corylus avellana

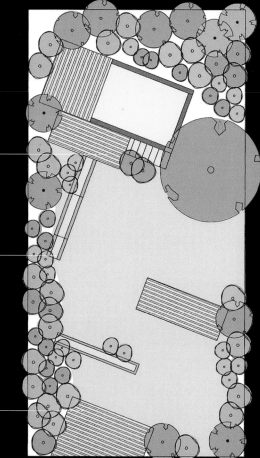

FINAL PLAN
Decking surrounded by lush lawn and planting provides sun terraces and dining areas

RAISED DECK
This elevated deck offers views across the garden

PAINTED RILL
A brilliant red rill channels water through the design

DINING AREA
A wooden patio area links the house to the rest of the garden

DETAILS

Building a wall, planting a hedge, or creating a border of some height directly across a garden creates intrigue, because you don't know what is going on behind it. An access point, such as a break in planting or a doorway, invites the visitor to continue their travels. A tantalizing glimpse of planting beyond, the tip of a structure, or the sound of water, also suggest that the journey in the garden is not complete. The greenhouse fulfills all these functions, creating a visual barrier but also offering a half-hidden view of the garden behind.

The building itself is a beautiful piece of architecture, as well as being very functional. One-third is clad in western red cedar with a stainless-steel roof, while the remaining walls and roof are glass. Where the glass roof arches down, the ground has been partially excavated into the hillside and lined with plastered concrete blocks to create a sunken greenhouse suitable for growing tender plants.

▲ RAW MATERIALS

ABOVE (THREE PICTURES) I used strips of stainless steel, more commonly found in restaurant kitchens, to clad one-third of the roof. Inside, the roof is lined with wood to create a warm, intimate space. The structure is held together with huge, curved girders. I particularly like the way the hard, cold metal contrasts with the warm cedar walls.

◄ INSIDE OUT

LEFT A square deck juts out from the greenhouse, extending the living space and blurring the distinction between outside and indoors. Exploiting the property's gentle slope, it offers an elevated view of the garden as the land sweeps down toward the house. A flight of wooden steps links the deck—which is held up by girders mirroring those used to build the glass structure—to the lawn below. I planted a rowan tree to one side of the deck, which will eventually help to shade it from the noon sun.

► THE BIGGER PICTURE

OPPOSITE PAGE (SIX PICTURES) As well as a great living space, the greenhouse makes a dramatic architectural statement, and divides the area between the trees at the back of the plot and the lawn in front.

It offers people protection from the elements, and is a great place to relax and view the garden. The sun quickly warms up the interior, while on hot days the wooden section of the building creates a shady retreat.

The long lawn is broken up with wooden decks that can be used for entertaining or sunbathing. Two bright red rills, one of which runs from under the greenhouse, and the other from beneath the borders, introduce splashes of color and create a brilliant contrast with the rich green lawn and borders.

The owners aren't avid gardeners, and the planting consists mainly of easy-care, structural plants, such as clipped boxwood balls, cotoneaster, and spiky-leaved phormiums.

This garden turned out to be one of my favorites because it remains true to a strong idea. My client, Jocelyn, had lived in her row house for about 20 years—she loved her long, narrow garden and enjoyed wandering through it. But although she was quite taken by what already existed there, she felt that there was no social space and that it lacked a design focus. I was asked to create something that made a blunt statement, using raw, modern materials, and unfussy, clean lines. My thoughts were immediate—framing views through cast-concrete windows.

INSPIRATIONS

Concrete dominated my vision for this garden. It was a familiar material to the Romans, but in recent times, it's been used to build everything from football stadiums and apartment blocks to park benches. Gray concrete dominates our urban landscape, and is thought of as a utilitarian product without any sense of beauty. But I disagree—when used well, it is an attractive, flexible material that is both practical and awe-inspiring. It also has limitless design capabilities, and can be manipulated, molded, sprayed, and shaped to create a huge range of beautiful forms.

Inspired by structures such as the Stadelhofen station in Zurich, and the arching roof of the bus garage in Stockwell, London, I knew I could create a stunning design with this material.

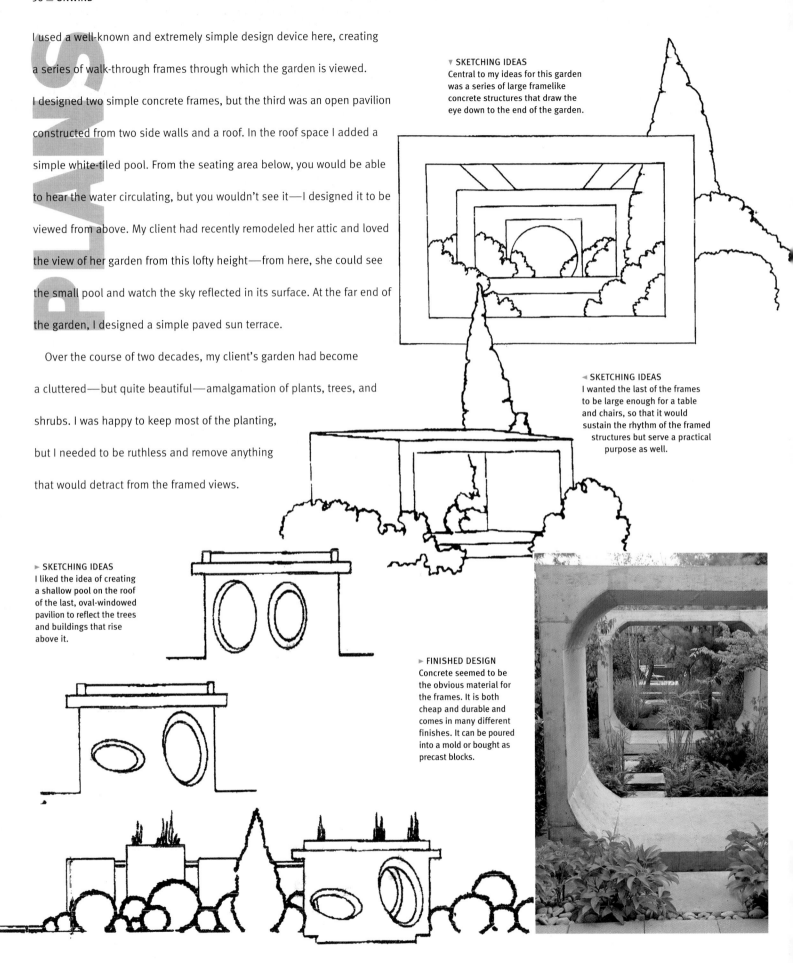

PLANS

I used a well-known and extremely simple design device here, creating

a series of walk-through frames through which the garden is viewed.

I designed two simple concrete frames, but the third was an open pavilion

constructed from two side walls and a roof. In the roof space I added a

simple white-tiled pool. From the seating area below, you would be able

to hear the water circulating, but you wouldn't see it—I designed it to be

viewed from above. My client had recently remodeled her attic and loved

the view of her garden from this lofty height—from here, she could see

the small pool and watch the sky reflected in its surface. At the far end of

the garden, I designed a simple paved sun terrace.

Over the course of two decades, my client's garden had become

a cluttered—but quite beautiful—amalgamation of plants, trees, and

shrubs. I was happy to keep most of the planting,

but I needed to be ruthless and remove anything

that would detract from the framed views.

▼ SKETCHING IDEAS
Central to my ideas for this garden
was a series of large framelike
concrete structures that draw the
eye down to the end of the garden.

◄ SKETCHING IDEAS
I wanted the last of the frames
to be large enough for a table
and chairs, so that it would
sustain the rhythm of the framed
structures but serve a practical
purpose as well.

► SKETCHING IDEAS
I liked the idea of creating
a shallow pool on the roof
of the last, oval-windowed
pavilion to reflect the trees
and buildings that rise
above it.

► FINISHED DESIGN
Concrete seemed to be
the obvious material for
the frames. It is both
cheap and durable and
comes in many different
finishes. It can be poured
into a mold or bought as
precast blocks.

I added a selection of mature trees and shrubs to supplement the existing planting in this garden. Using big plants gives instantaneous results, but you do have to make sure you have the right conditions for them to thrive. You also have to look after them extremely well for the first few years, never stinting on watering, feeding, and general care. If you decide to treat yourself to a few mature trees, make sure you have extra help, because even if you use lifting equipment, you will still need to do the final maneuvering by hand.

Green was to be the dominant planting color, with plenty of texture and form between the solid concrete frames. Our chosen plants—*Rhus typhina*, liquidambar, *Euonymus alatus*, birch (*Betula*), and pine—rely on leaf shape, bark, and green foliage to provide interest. A small pool between two of the frames was planted with a low-maintenance mix of papyrus (*Cyperus papyrus*) and oxygenating plants.

PLANTING LIST

CLOCKWISE FROM TOP LEFT

Betula utilis var. *jacquemontii*
Cyperus papyrus
Polypodium vulgare
Helleborus argutifolius
Rhus typhina
Polystichum setiferum Divisilobum Group
Pinus mugo 'Mops'

FINAL PLAN
This garden has a single, simple theme: framing views

SUN TERRACE
The patio at the end of the garden is the perfect spot to catch the sun

GREEN SPACE
The lawn creates a breathing space between the concrete squares

SOFT EDGES
Groups of ferns soften the edges of the hard landscaping

ALIGNED FRAMES
All three concrete frames are in perfect alignment— the first one was used as a sighting line

SHRUBBY INTRO
A line of architectural plants fills the

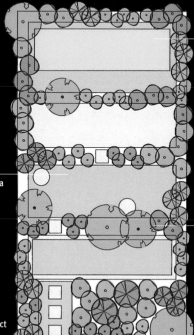

The huge concrete frames were made off-site, then hoisted over the roof of my client's row house into the back garden. The city gave me permission to close off a side road for a day while the structures were brought in and lifted by a massive crane onto the waiting foundations.

For me, this was the most incredible part of the whole operation. The skill of the crane driver was simply awe-inspiring: through careful communication with the site manager, he was able to drop these massive concrete frames into exactly the right position, despite not seeing what was going on because his view was obstructed by the house. Time was short, and the team had had to plant up the garden, build the end terrace, lay the lawn, and dig out the pools before the structures arrived, so it was imperative that nothing was damaged during this process.

The client was overjoyed with the final garden design, and I love it, too. I stayed true to a simple concept and, in my experience, it is the simplest ideas that translate into the most effective garden designs. Bold and dramatic, this garden has received a lot of positive feedback, and overturned many people's perceptions of concrete. When used to pave over a green landscape, it can be abhorrent, but its smooth, cool texture provides the most beautiful backdrop to lush, sensuous planting.

DETAILS

◄ FRAMING THE VIEW

OPPOSITE PAGE (FOUR PICTURES)
An alignment of large concrete frames creates the illusion of greater length, drawing visitors down the garden to the sunny terrace at the end. The concrete used for these structures has a smooth, stonelike quality that provides a wonderful foil for the textural planting between them. The frame farthest from the house is a sheltered pavilion with a shallow pool on the roof that catches the light and reflects the sky. Resting on one of the concrete and steel benches, you can enjoy the view framed by the oval windows.

▲ IN PERSPECTIVE

ABOVE Seen from above, the dramatic geometry of the frames becomes even more apparent.

► FLOWING SHAPES

RIGHT I love the pavilion's oval windows—their flowing shape contrasts well with the sharp edges of the structures and furniture.

► OLD AND NEW

FAR RIGHT Creating a wonderful juxtaposition between old and new, the client's brick Victorian row house is neatly framed by the concrete structures.

Majestic trees, rustling grasses, waxy leaves, and velvet petals glistening with rain—these are just some of the riches to be found in natural gardens

NATURE

Fiona and her daughter Honey had a garden that, for me, was like a dream— very simple and very beautiful. A paved terrace led to lawn that, in turn, brought you to a cedar tree and, beyond that, a small wooded area. It was a real haven, and I questioned the idea of doing anything at all. But Fiona felt it lacked something. She wanted somewhere to enjoy nature, a place to chill, to relax, to socialize. In the end, I have tried to preserve the spirit of the garden by simply adding a wooden den set on stilts, which meant I barely had to touch a blade of grass.

SYLVAN

American architecture of the 1950s was a major inspiration for the wooden den. I also looked at timber-framed long-houses from Indonesia and buildings raised on stilts. Stilt houses skim over the ground without interfering with their surrounding environment, whether it's sea or savanna, and they offered me a way of keeping the garden intact. I also wanted the den to be screened off, to create a semi-private space. I imagined a building with sleek modern lines, but built with ancient, time-tested materials that would enhance, not detract, from the magical woodland garden.

Inside the den, I envisioned a North African setting. I had visited Morocco and was inspired by its courtyard gardens, but it was in Marrakesh that the idea of a suspended bed surrounded by jeweled lamps came to me.

INSPIRATIONS

PLANS

Fiona loved the plants and trees in her garden, but felt that as a whole, the space just wasn't working for her. What she really wanted was somewhere to relax, a place that would be cozy enough for one, but large enough to comfortably accommodate a group of friends.

Taking the cedar tree in the middle of the plot as a focal point, I decided to build a pavilion nearby that stretched from one boundary to the other, cutting the site in half. The area between the house and the pavilion would be lawn, with the original woodland behind. I also designed a wooden deck to replace the old concrete patio outside the house.

Inspired by the magical shapes, forms, and textures of North Africa, I wanted the whole building to light up at night like an exotic Moroccan lantern. And because the pavilion had to become part of its woodland surroundings, there could be no glass, just stainless-steel mesh—which reflects light in the most wonderful way. Mesh doesn't retain heat, but the fireplace I planned to include would ensure that the structure could be used year-round.

▲ ORIGINAL GARDEN
The garden was bordered by mature trees but the center was relatively open.

▼ SKETCHING IDEAS
The client wanted a space to relax in. It had to provide protection from the elements but not close visitors off from the surrounding woodland garden.

▼ FINISHED DESIGN
A mature cedar dominated the center of the garden and determined where the pavilion should be built.

▲ MODEL GARDEN
The stainless-steel mesh doors on either side of the room slide open to reveal the interior, which includes a brick fireplace and a bed suspended from the ceiling.

The moment I set foot in this urban garden, I had a very strong feeling that it was, in fact, one slice of an older, larger plot—the mature cedar and a very old wall both gave me the hunch. The space already featured some lovely planting, which both Fiona and I were determined to keep. This included a woodland area toward the back of the yard, beautifully carpeted with various ivies, to which I added some new species. My main contribution to the structural planting was five tree ferns (dicksonias)—at the back where Honey and her friends like to play— and some Japanese maples (acers), but I also introduced other ferns, and a smattering of pretty geraniums and foxgloves. Some time after the garden was finished, Fiona held a child-naming ceremony. It was a truly magical experience, watching the children gathered under the tree ferns listening to a storyteller, with the sun streaming through the fronds.

PLANTS

PLANTING LIST

CLOCKWISE FROM TOP LEFT
Dryopteris filix-mas
Acer palmatum var. *dissectum* 'Garnet'
Geranium 'Johnson's Blue'
Hedera helix 'Eva'
Epimedium x *versicolor* 'Sulphureum'
Digitalis purpurea
Cedrus atlantica Glauca Group

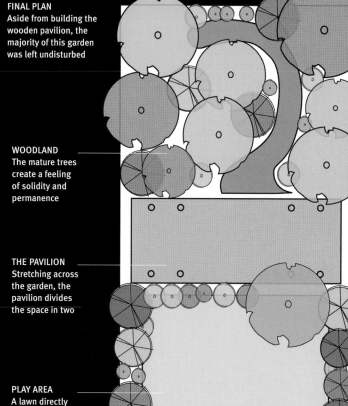

FINAL PLAN
Aside from building the wooden pavilion, the majority of this garden was left undisturbed

WOODLAND
The mature trees create a feeling of solidity and permanence

THE PAVILION
Stretching across the garden, the pavilion divides the space in two

PLAY AREA
A lawn directly outside the house provides a space for children to play

DETAILS

I loved this garden as it was, but Fiona wanted me to "make sense" of it, and I knew what she meant. It needed some kind of structure, however organic-looking, to create a garden that she could use, and not just look at. Having finalized the plan for a large pavilion, I decided that it was important not to damage any of the existing planting, not so much as a blade of grass, during construction. This was not only so that the plants could continue to thrive, but also because the moment the building was finished, I wanted the design to look as though it had always been there. We therefore constructed a temporary raised scaffolding walkway above the whole plot for builders and other site visitors to use. The pavilion itself was relatively easy to build. It is constructed around eight telephone poles that support the floor and roof. Lastly, Fiona asked for a skylight—not in my original plan—to be installed to fill the room with dappled light.

◄ MIRRORING NATURE

OPPOSITE PAGE TOP (TWO PICTURES) Stretched across the garden, the structure is designed to meld unobtrusively into the sylvan setting. The wooden framework and the telephone poles used to support it all mirror the surrounding trees.

Sliding doors on each side of the room provide protection against the harsher autumn and winter elements, while on warm spring or hot summer days, they can be pulled back to allow a through breeze.

◄ FOCAL POINT

OPPOSITE PAGE FAR LEFT The mellow brick fireplace is a real asset; it provides a beautiful focal point, and allows Fiona to enjoy the room throughout the year.

Set in this wooded environment, the heated room also offers wonderful views of the trees as they change with the seasons. When designing the interior, I imagined friends gathered around for drinks at Christmas—the scent of wet leaves and wood smoke filling the air—or Fiona relaxing with a book on a Sunday afternoon.

◄ WOODLAND SANCTUARY

OPPOSITE PAGE LEFT Opposite the fireplace, a day bed is suspended by chains from the ceiling. Covered with a soft mattress and scattered with cushions, this hammocklike divan is perfect for a nap.

A bed is a great addition to a garden room—so relaxing and so romantic. I imagine drifting off to sleep on a warm day to the sounds of birds singing in the trees. At night, the soft glow of the Moroccan-style lanterns adds to the dreamy, romantic scene.

▲ A GENTLE TOUCH

ABOVE My initial reaction to this garden was to walk away and leave it untouched, but having agreed with the client to work on it, I was adamant that the building I finally imposed did not detract from its natural beauty. Fundamental to the design were the materials used in the construction. Clay bricks and wooden floors and walls echo the colors and textures of the trees. The mesh panels in the doors allow fresh garden scents to filter into the room.

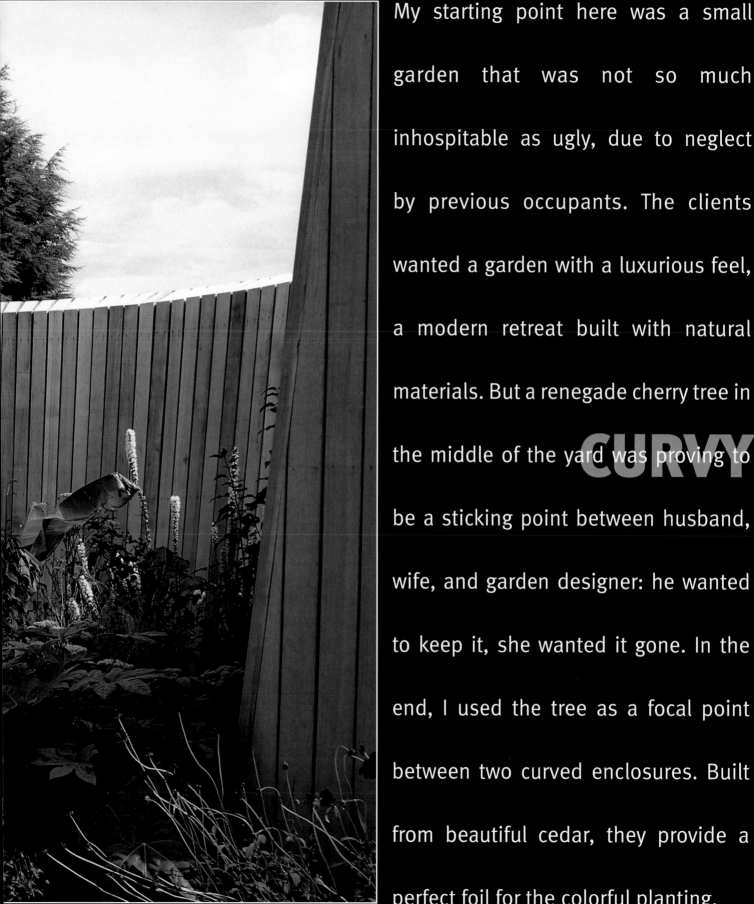

My starting point here was a small garden that was not so much inhospitable as ugly, due to neglect by previous occupants. The clients wanted a garden with a luxurious feel, a modern retreat built with natural materials. But a renegade cherry tree in the middle of the yard was proving to be a sticking point between husband, wife, and garden designer: he wanted to keep it, she wanted it gone. In the end, I used the tree as a focal point between two curved enclosures. Built from beautiful cedar, they provide a perfect foil for the colorful planting.

INSPIRATIONS

A sensual exploration of the human form was key to my design for this garden. The curvaceous shapes of the structures are inspired by reclining figures: buns, backs, and breasts. I visualized a fluid wooden structure, with sheer sides resembling the "wall of death" at a fair.

Beautiful and durable western red cedar was chosen for the construction. While in Vancouver, on the west coast of Canada, I had seen the trees being harvested, and learned of their use in both traditional and contemporary architecture. The wood, which falls somewhere between softwood and hardwood, has natural oils that make it resistant to pests and diseases. It can either be left in its natural state, or oiled or stained to retain its warm appearance.

As a foil for the wood, I chose dark-hued plants from a specialist plant catalog.

My aim was to devise a coherent plan that would center around the cherry, and convince the client that keeping the tree was the right decision. I also wanted to replace the existing ugly and rather haphazard boundaries—which consisted of a few yards of hedging with some concrete post-and-panel fencing—with sculptural shapes that would enclose the garden and also work in their own right as features.

My plan was to build two enclosures, constructed from cedar, in almost connecting C-shapes. They would both meet under the canopy of the tree and be linked by a curved wooden ramp. The enclosure farthest from the house would include a lawn, offset by granite cobble pavers, and a bench seat. I imagined grassy and straplike foliage adorning this area. The enclosure closest to the house was also designed as a seating area, and would play host to dark, sumptuous foliage plants in a curved bed. I chose cream stone paving to contrast with the wood and planting, and in the shade under the cherry tree, I designed a ferny grove.

PLANS

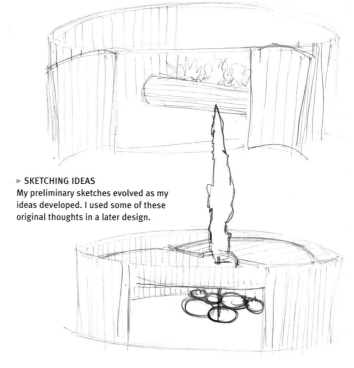

► SKETCHING IDEAS
My preliminary sketches evolved as my ideas developed. I used some of these original thoughts in a later design.

◄ FINISHED DESIGN
Warm-looking, honey-colored cedar was used to create the gently curving walls of both enclosures.

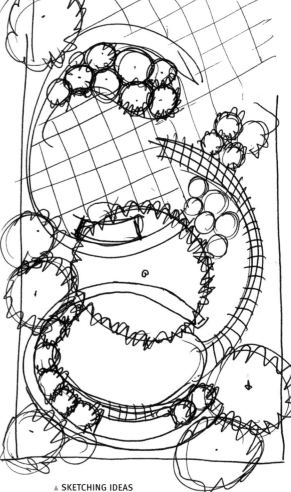

▲ SKETCHING IDEAS
As the sketches developed, two enclosed areas—built on either side of a mature cherry tree—emerged.

The client wanted dark, luxurious plants, which I bought from a specialist nursery run by Derry Watkins, who is an engaging and very knowledgeable plantswoman. With her help, we picked a wonderful selection of toned foliage plants that look stunning against the cedar walls and create a haven for family and wildlife.

My particular favorite is *Canna* 'Wyoming', a slightly tender plant that in a frosty garden would have to be overwintered inside, but will survive outside in these sheltered enclosures. I also teamed the grass *Imperata cylindrica* 'Rubra', which throws up flames of red foliage in summer, with the blood-red flowers and smoldering dark leaves of the dahlia 'Bishop of Llandaff'. A lovely purple-leaved hazel (*Corylus maxima* 'Purpurea') and Boston ivy with smoky foliage (*Parthenocissus tricuspidata* 'Veitchii') add a vertical dimension to my planting plan.

PLANTS

PLANTING LIST

CLOCKWISE FROM TOP LEFT

Ophiopogon planiscapus 'Nigrescens'
Canna 'Wyoming'
Heuchera 'Palace Purple Select'
Imperata cylindrica 'Rubra'
Parthenocissus tricuspidata 'Veitchii'
Corylus maxima 'Purpurea'
Dahlia 'Bishop of Llandaff'

FINAL PLAN
The garden's enclosures sweep around and are linked together by the cherry tree

COBBLED PATH
A rough cobbled area defines the circular lawn

LINKING PATH
Curved wooden decking provides a link between the two enclosures

SHELTER BELT
Planting is well protected from strong winds by the curved walls

DETAILS

The quality of the craftsmanship was key to the beauty of the enclosures in this garden. The structures themselves have an internal skeleton of steel and are clad in cedar. Every length of timber was hand-cut to create the curved walls, which flare out slightly at the bottom, and the structures had to be carefully constructed to ensure that they sit clear of the ground, so that surface water doesn't rot the wood.

This is one of my most successful gardens: crafted to the highest standard and simple in design, it works well on both an aesthetic level and a practical level. The wooden walls of the enclosures radiate heat, leaving their occupants feeling relaxed, warm, and secure, even during the winter months. The colors are also beautiful and natural: the honey tones of the wood balance the cream Portland stone paving, and the soft grays of the cobble pavers work brilliantly against the smooth, emerald lawn in the second enclosure.

▲ SHELF LIFE

TOP The cedar walls of the enclosures soak up heat and make a warm backrest for the seats.

The wooden bench here is set, shelflike, into the smooth curve of the wall, and offers a resting place where the owners can sit, relax, and enjoy the tropical planting.

To create a magical atmosphere at night, I have inset tiny lights into the wooden walls to wash the dark foliage plants with a soft blue hue.

▲ TACTILE TEXTURES

ABOVE (FOUR PICTURES) One of the main themes of this garden is texture. Often overlooked at the expense of color, texture can create just as much excitement and drama.

Smooth warm wood, hard edgy concrete—used here to make the seat in the second enclosure—sharp spiky phormium and miscanthus leaves, boldly veined heuchera foliage, and rough cobbles combine to create a garden that feels as good as it looks.

► PIVOTAL CHERRY

OPPOSITE PAGE MAIN PICTURE The old cherry tree that occupied the center of the original garden layout now acts as the fulcrum on which the two circular rooms seem to balance. In a small, confined space such as this, I could see the tree's potential as a design device: look up through the canopy and the sky offers a view of infinite space, in contrast to the insular enclosures. The shade it affords also helps to cool the garden on sunny days.

► LOFTY ILLUSIONS

OPPOSITE PAGE FAR RIGHT (FOUR PICTURES) To make the enclosures, each plank of cedar had to be cut individually to create the wedge-shaped walls. The wood was then fixed to a steel frame. The shape of the structures makes them appear taller than they are when you look up at them—the tree adds to this illusion.

Some of the exotic architectural plants are tender but safe from frosts in their warm, sheltered beds.

Despite being overlooked by an apartment building, this tree-lined garden felt like a place apart when I first saw it. The clients have three children, and my brief was to create a family garden that reflected the woodland nature of the site, yet was also an exciting and vibrant place for children to play in. The couple—she's a New Zealander and he's British—had spent a lot of time abroad and wanted me to include plants that reflected their travels. So I used natural materials for the paths and den, softened by exotic and native New Zealand plants.

INSPIRATIONS

My inspirations for this garden were varied: birch trees from a bog in Leitrim in Ireland; the hull of a boat; and cedar shingles, which, in time, turn from a deep red color to sun-bleached white.

I wanted to create a garden of movement, with strong lines and shapes, dominated by plants. Uppermost in my mind was a place for people to gather together and talk, but one that was unusual and fun, too.

For the garden lighting I was eager to create a sense of mystery. I'd seen an installation in east London called "Holding Pattern," in which blue blobs of light shone out from the top of tall, thin silver poles. They reminded me of tall matchsticks, or lights on the back of a police motorcycle. I decided to use these in groups of five, shooting out of the ground at varying heights and angles. At night, the tiny lights would appear to hover magically.

PLANS

My plan developed with an oval-shaped, slightly raised deck leading out from the back of the house. In front of this, I sketched an oval lawn that dipped in the center, almost like a saucer, and led to an S-shaped pathway. Constructed of cedar, it was to be fixed to a metal frame that curved and cambered gracefully through the garden.

Movement was key, and the swerving path gave the garden pace and excitement. Its route skirted an existing cherry tree, circled a planned bog bed, passed by a massive, ornate sphere, and eventually led to a garden room made from cedar shingles that nestled in a fairly secluded, woodland area at the bottom of the garden.

The gentle shapes and natural materials blended into existing wooded areas. And the beautiful plants, which I squeezed into every available space on my plan, would give the garden a lush, fresh look.

▲ SKETCHING IDEAS
The clients wanted an outdoor room that they could use as an office. I decided to build this at the very back of the garden, well away from the noise of the house.

◄ FINISHED DESIGN
A large metal sphere was placed among the plants to act as a sculptural focal point and echo the flowing lines of the design.

▲ SKETCHING IDEAS
This garden is defined by circles and gently arching forms nestling among the textures and colors of the planting.

I made sure there was loads of room for plants, including exotics such as tree ferns, which complement the grasses, sedges, and woodrushes that I have included. A bog garden in the center plays host to *Gunnera manicata*, *Acorus gramineus* 'Ogon', and other moisture-loving plants. Birch trees are useful for screening areas of the garden without throwing it into deep shade, since their feathery canopies allow light to filter through. A feeling of depth and interest is created by bringing specimen plants, such as the wonderful twisted weeping willow, *Salix babylonica* var. *pekinensis* 'Tortuosa', to the fore.

Autumn and winter interest in the garden is sustained by the startling fruits of *Callicarpa bodinieri* var. *giraldii* 'Profusion', *Euonymus europaeus* 'Red Cascade', *Sorbus commixta* 'Embley', and the guelder rose, *Viburnum opulus*. Together, these provide purple, red, and orange bursts of color throughout the garden.

PLANTS

PLANTING LIST

CLOCKWISE FROM TOP LEFT

Miscanthus sinensis 'Gracillimus'
Spiraea japonica 'Goldflame'
Sorbus commixta 'Embley'
Mahonia aquifolium 'Smaragd'
Vinca minor 'La Grave'
Cornus alba 'Aurea'
Deschampsia caespitosa

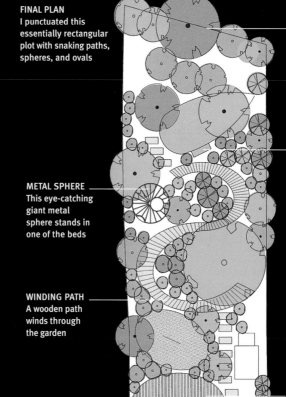

FINAL PLAN
I punctuated this essentially rectangular plot with snaking paths, spheres, and ovals

EXISTING PLANTS
Mature plants and trees were retained at the back of the garden

WORK SPACE
The office, built at the end of the plot, looks like an upside-down boat

METAL SPHERE
This eye-catching giant metal sphere stands in one of the beds

WINDING PATH
A wooden path winds through the garden

SUN DECK
Attached to the house is an oval patio

DETAILS

The end of this garden was overlooked by apartments, so creating privacy was an important part of my clients' brief. I developed the idea of an outdoor den to block them out—it would also screen some ugly walling and fencing. Half hidden by the surrounding plants—gentle and wispy, as befits a woodland garden—the den is quite hard to see. Its rounded shape was inspired by the hulls of boats stored upside-down on beaches. The circular structure in the middle of the den looks like the entrance but is, in fact, a window; the doorway is on the side.

A large metal sphere was designed for family get-togethers, the idea being that they can throw a load of cushions inside, climb in, and sit down to talk. The cage is great for lounging around in and doesn't move because of its enormous weight. Carefully positioned under an existing hazel, it immediately looked at home. The bog beds, family cage, and den are all linked by a winding wooden pathway.

▲ RUSTIC APPEARANCE

ABOVE The den was constructed around a metal frame covered with several layers of wood. The wood was then coated with a rubberized solution and clad with rustic-looking cedar shingles. I decided to leave the den empty of furnishings so that the family could use it exactly as they wanted.

◄ HARD AND SOFT

LEFT Simplicity and family fun are key elements in this garden. Set in a bed close to the boat-shaped den is a large metal sphere made of curved metal strips. Designed to be used as a sort of family room, I envisioned parents and children throwing in piles of soft cushions and lounging around talking and laughing together.

The hard landscaping in the garden—including the den and the sphere—provides both solid and more delicate, semi-transparent backdrops against which the abundance of textured plants, with their colored foliage, work extremely well.

► NATURAL FANTASY

OPPOSITE PAGE (SIX PICTURES) This was a gentle design for people who were a little bit scared of anything too modern or out of this world. They wanted architecture in the garden but nothing harsh, and they definitely didn't want spaceships! The design evolved into a sort of natural fantasy garden—it's quite soft and intriguing, and reminds me of a Hobbit's garden in The Lord of the Rings.

The native planting of silver birches, sedges, rushes, and ferns—whose colors and forms change so dramatically through the seasons—brings the yard to life, bursting from the beds to create eye-catching points of interest.

Foliage plays a vital part in the planting. I chose varieties with strong-colored leaves—from fresh to sage green to yellow to red and purple, as well as silver and gold—and distinctive leaf shapes—broad and palmate, small and needlelike, or delicate and finely divided.

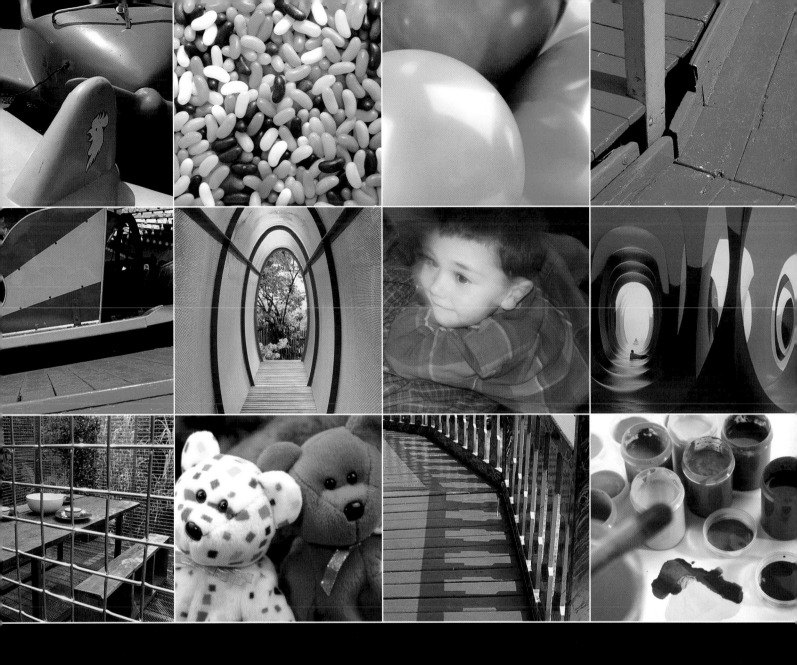

Silver rockets, giant purple eggs, and candy-colored spinning tops are features **PLAY** of these gardens where kids can have fun

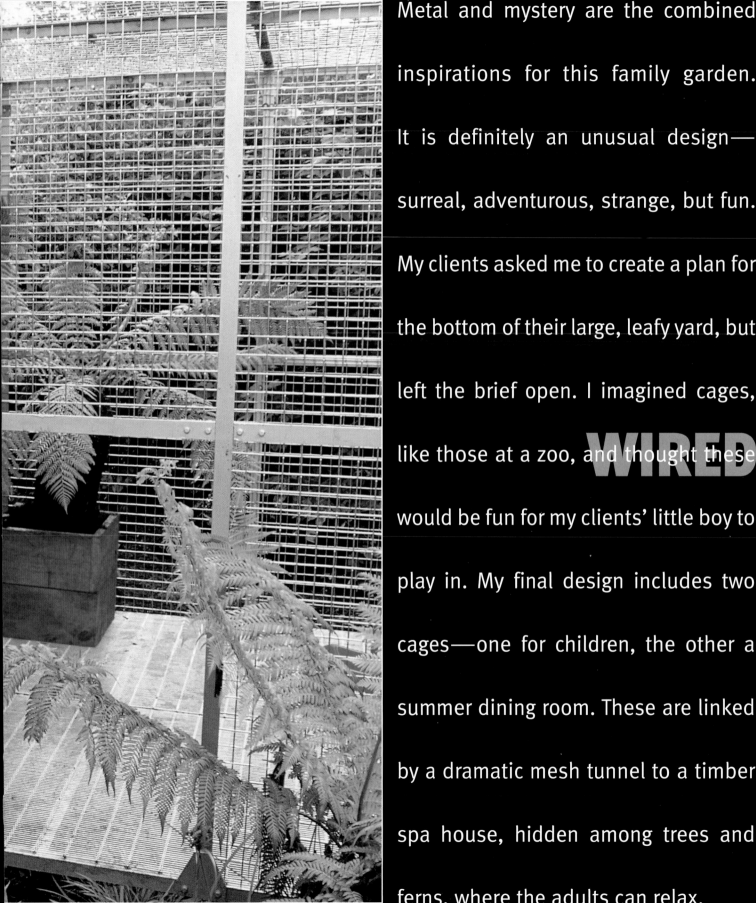

Metal and mystery are the combined inspirations for this family garden. It is definitely an unusual design— surreal, adventurous, strange, but fun. My clients asked me to create a plan for the bottom of their large, leafy yard, but left the brief open. I imagined cages, like those at a zoo, and thought these would be fun for my clients' little boy to play in. My final design includes two cages—one for children, the other a summer dining room. These are linked by a dramatic mesh tunnel to a timber spa house, hidden among trees and ferns, where the adults can relax.

WIRED

INSPIRATIONS

I had great fun with this garden, as the clients gave me free rein to be at my most surreal. References included the way Damien Hirst frames a snapshot of life and displays it in a tank of formaldehyde. I hate to see live animals in cages, and with my twisted sense of humor, I wondered what it would be like if the roles were reversed and we were put on display instead. I saw a picture of a wildlife park in New York where kids, enclosed in see-through tubes, become the exhibits, and thought of aquariums where the fish swim over your head—who is the viewer, who is being watched? An image of Desperate Dan's chin jutting through the bars of the jailhouse kept springing to mind, too, but that kind of enclosure was too extreme. I wanted something that wouldn't look out of place in a natural history program, like a giant aviary or terrarium in a natural, jungly setting.

There was space in the garden for two massive cages, and I designed one three yards square, and the other four yards square. I thought the larger of the two would make a fantastic, semi-enclosed family patio, complete with table, bench, and plants in pots. The smaller cage would be perfect as a children's playroom. I sketched climbers, planted at the base of each cube, with the idea that they would, in time, partially cover the structures.

My plan also included a futuristic tunnel, created by wrapping stainless-steel mesh over a series of elliptical frames. This tunnel would dissect a forest of tree ferns, and lead to a Japanese-style bathhouse—complete with a luxurious sunken bath made of poured concrete—where the adults could relax. The bathhouse would have mesh-screen walls that could swivel open and shut for extra privacy. I decided to use reclaimed wood for the rest of the bathhouse, and to raise it on sturdy telephone poles.

▲ SKETCHING IDEAS
Although the cubes I sketched were large enough to be used as garden rooms, their wire-mesh design prevents them from becoming too dominant or oppressive.

► MODEL GARDEN
The tunnel traverses a bog garden and an area planted with tree ferns. The mesh-covered structure has a slatted wood floor and is raised above the plants on legs.

◄ FINISHED DESIGN
The cages create a sense of privacy, partially screening the foliage and flowers outside.

PLANTS

I created a massive bog garden by excavating the central area of the garden to a depth of 24in (60cm). Then, having lined the hole with a PVC pond liner, I refilled it with a mix of soil, manure, and compost. Charcoal was also added to keep the soil smelling sweet. The bed is planted with ligularias, rodgersias, rheums, gunneras, astilbes, hostas, and primulas. Bog garden plants like these are fast growers and fill out in a surprisingly short space of time—perfect for creating a jungle setting around the tunnel and walkways. This type of planting is typically seen at the edge of water in woodland areas and isn't really suitable as an overall theme in a garden. It also dies down over winter.

I treated the cages like cubed trellis, draping them with grapevines, which would be heavy with sun-ripened fruit in autumn, and wisteria, whose purple flowers would cover the mesh walls in late spring.

PLANTING LIST

CLOCKWISE FROM TOP LEFT
Carex elata 'Aurea'
Gunnera manicata
Ligularia dentata 'Desdemona'
Betula utilis var. *jacquemontii*
Hebe rakaiensis
Ficus carica
Dicksonia antarctica

FINAL PLAN
Features are set on the diagonal in this garden to make the most of the rectangular space

WIRE TUNNEL
The raised, mesh tunnel leads to the bathhouse and allows good views of the bog garden plants below

PLANTING
Existing mature trees are combined with new tree ferns and birches

WIRE CAGES
The garden's wire cages are placed in close proximity to each other

For a suburban garden, I had a lot of land to play with—a luxury that allowed me to divide the space up quite dramatically into distinct and separate areas. The wire-mesh tunnel that links these together acts a little like a gauze curtain pulled across a room, dividing and screening the garden but allowing a veiled glimpse of planting and features on the other side of it. The tunnel is elevated, as are the cages, and together they form a continuous raised surface around the garden. Even a slight elevation offers a different perspective, and as you walk through the site you get a wonderful overview of the planting.

The big yard also allowed me to indulge my passion for architectural plants—their foliage creates wonderful shadows across the mesh screens. In fact, one of the joys of this site for me was the shafts of light filtering through the different textures. At night, the blue spotlights trained onto the walkways give them an extraterrestrial feel.

▲ LIVING ROOMS

ABOVE (FOUR PICTURES) Large wire cages with metal grille floors are used to create raised garden rooms that literally come alive as the existing planting curls around the bars and pushes between the mesh. I like the effect of the hard surfaces knitting together with the soft planting.

◄ CASTING SHADOWS

FAR LEFT Even diffused light casts shadows through the mesh of the tunnel onto the wooden floor. Cutting across the bog garden beside a bed of architectural plants—including an already large but potentially giant gunnera—the tunnel looks as though it has been lifted straight off the set of a science-fiction movie.

◄ SEMI-TRANSPARENT

LEFT (TWO PICTURES) With the roof supported by telephone poles, one entire wall of the spa room is made up of framed, semi-transparent mesh panels that pivot to open and close.

► TUNNEL VISION

OPPOSITE PAGE MAIN PICTURE The fronds of the tree ferns press up against the sides of the tunnel, heralding the entrance to the walkway. One of the most successful features of the garden, in my view, is the framed vista through this tunnel.

► OPEN TO THE ELEMENTS

OPPOSITE PAGE (REMAINING 10 PICTURES) There are two wire rooms: one is a children's playroom, and the other a summer dining room that's perfect for entertaining. The wire mesh used in the construction of the rooms and the tunnels varies in texture and gauge, and gives the different areas of the garden an individual look and personality. But because they are all made from the same material, the design has coherence.

The bathhouse is really luxurious, with its hot shower and sunken, concrete bath. The bath may not be to everyone's taste, but I love its urban look.

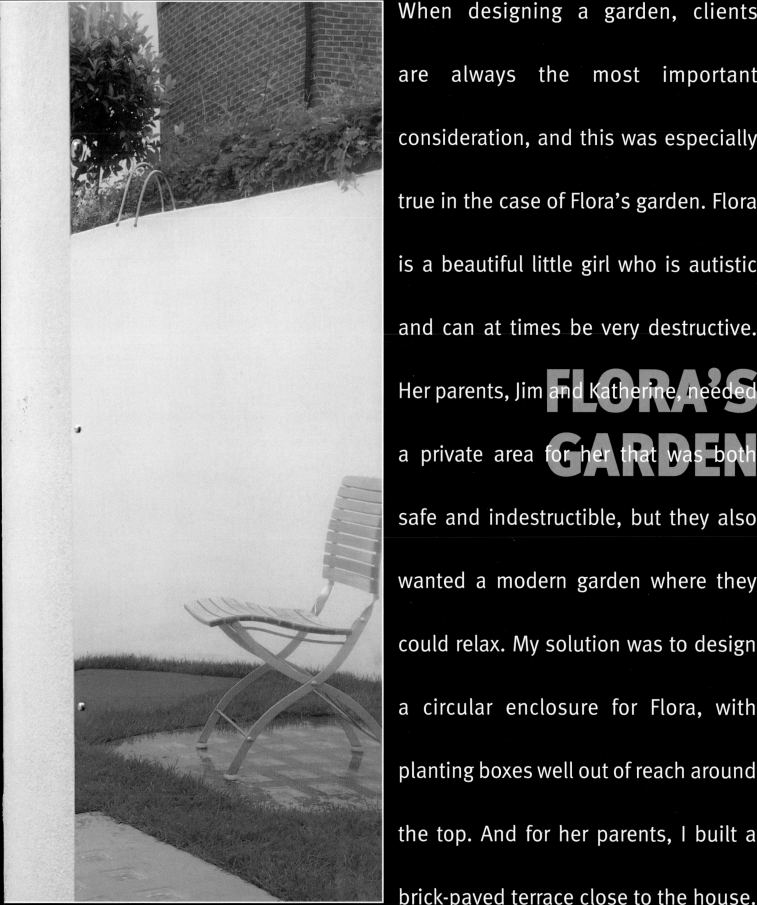

When designing a garden, clients are always the most important consideration, and this was especially true in the case of Flora's garden. Flora is a beautiful little girl who is autistic and can at times be very destructive.

FLORA'S GARDEN

Her parents, Jim and Katherine, needed a private area for her that was both safe and indestructible, but they also wanted a modern garden where they could relax. My solution was to design a circular enclosure for Flora, with planting boxes well out of reach around the top. And for her parents, I built a brick-paved terrace close to the house.

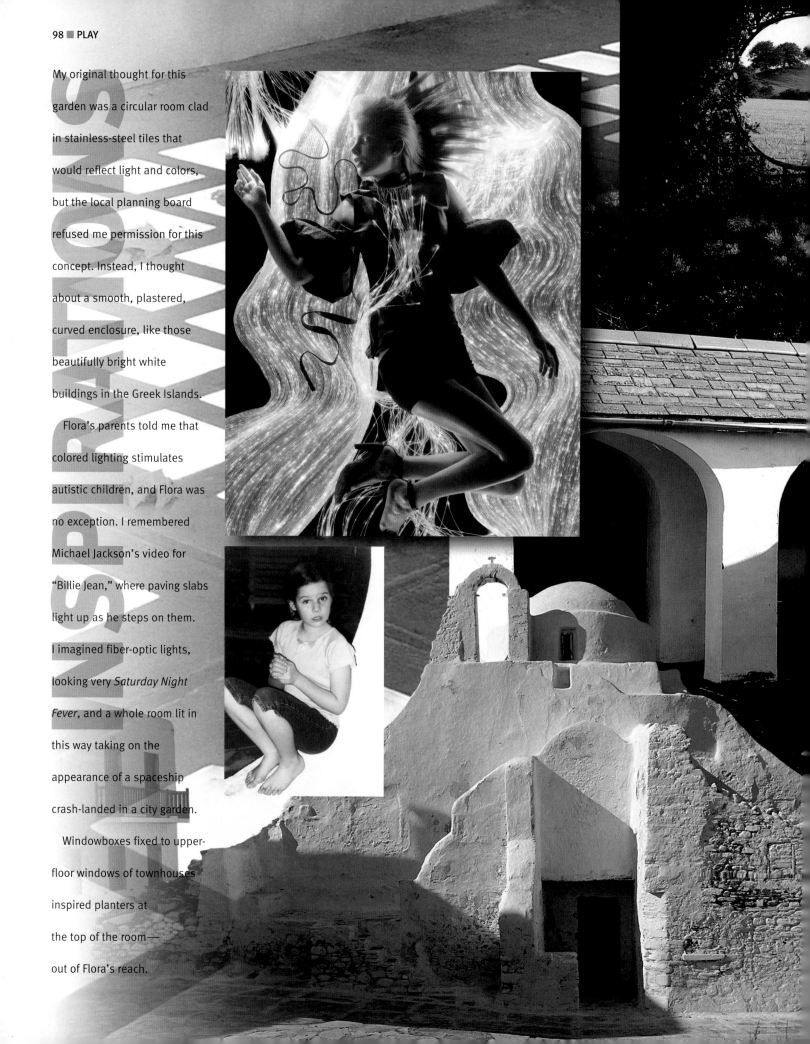

INSPIRATIONS

My original thought for this garden was a circular room clad in stainless-steel tiles that would reflect light and colors, but the local planning board refused me permission for this concept. Instead, I thought about a smooth, plastered, curved enclosure, like those beautifully bright white buildings in the Greek Islands.

Flora's parents told me that colored lighting stimulates autistic children, and Flora was no exception. I remembered Michael Jackson's video for "Billie Jean," where paving slabs light up as he steps on them. I imagined fiber-optic lights, looking very *Saturday Night Fever*, and a whole room lit in this way taking on the appearance of a spaceship crash-landed in a city garden.

Windowboxes fixed to upper-floor windows of townhouses inspired planters at the top of the room—out of Flora's reach.

To create a more hospitable space, I decided to break up the long, thin, rectangular yard with a circular room. I designed the room, which is built in plastered concrete block, as wide as possible. In places I planned double-skinned walls with a 30in (75cm) cavity in between, and designed windowboxes set into the top for small shrubs, trees, grasses, and climbers. At 7ft (2.3m) above ground, the windowboxes would be out of Flora's reach, and would offer the unusual experience of looking up at foliage and flowers from below. The clients also needed a shed, so just behind the circular enclosure I planned a long, curved storage room. The "shed room" also features raised planters at the top, and an aquarium at one end for Kyle, Flora's older brother.

I designed a brick patio area close to the house for the adults, with the pavers laid on the diagonal to make the area seem wider. Then, to add a textural and visual contrast, I inset strips of different-colored brick in a diamond pattern. I also included a set of gates between the patio and the room, to keep Flora in the central play area where she would be safe.

PLANS

► MODEL GARDEN
Flora's circular enclosure spans the width of the garden, and a large round window frames the view inside.

◄ FINISHED DESIGN
Concrete slabs inset with colored glass and lit from below, and projected images of cartoons, create a fun nighttime garden for Flora.

◄ ORIGINAL GARDEN
Flora's parents wanted to transform their drab garden into a stimulating yet safe space for their daughter.

► SKETCHING IDEAS
I came up with the idea of an open-topped enclosure edged with flower beds that were well out of Flora's grasp.

Flora loves the look of plants, but would rip them out of the ground if she could get hold of them. This meant that all the planting had to be in the raised boxes at the top of the circular enclosure and shed, apart from a few sturdy shrubs and trees that I planted in pots on the patio.

Despite this restriction, I have packed a huge array of beautiful plants into the garden. Clematis and vines (*Vitis coignetiae*), which normally grow upward, look stunning cascading down the plastered walls. Flora's love of color is factored in to the planting plan, too. Bright yellow and magenta achilleas, pink feathery astilbes, and deep blue ajugas rub shoulders with pencil-thin Italian cypress trees to produce a montage of colors, shapes, and textures.

In the pots, I have planted a photinia, an evergreen that has lovely red-tinted young foliage in spring, and *Cercis canadensis* 'Forest Pansy', a beautiful small tree with heart-shaped, dark red leaves.

PLANTS

PLANTING LIST

CLOCKWISE FROM TOP LEFT

Wisteria floribunda 'Multijuga'
Achillea 'Moonshine'
Ajuga reptans 'Multicolor'
Astilbe 'Aphrodite'
Vitis coignetiae
Cercis canadensis 'Forest Pansy'
Clematis armandii 'Snowdrift'

WORKING PLAN
This garden is divided into separate areas. Slight alterations were made in the final construction

CURVED SHED
This structure houses a shed and an aquarium for Kyle

RAISED BEDS
The gap between the double walls offers space for planters at the top

PAVING LIGHTS
Concrete paving slabs inset with colored glass light up after dark

PATIO PLANTING
Small trees and large shrubs are set into containers on the patio

PAVING PATTERN
The brick paving is laid diagonally to increase the feeling of width

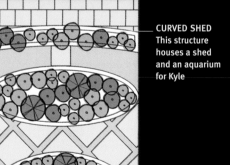

DETAILS

Flora's house and garden are historic structures and are protected by the local planning commission from any development that is deemed detrimental to their original character. This limited my options for the circular room, but the white-walled enclosures were acceptable.

White surfaces work well in both hot and temperate countries, and even under a gray sky, they reflect light into the garden. In this context, the enclosures also disguise the boundaries and shelter the property from neighboring yards.

On a practical note, great thought had to be put into constructing the raised planters. An automatic watering system was installed so that the clients can easily keep the plants in peak condition during the summer. Drainage holes were also created in the walls of the enclosure to prevent the planters from becoming waterlogged. The plants do require a little maintenance in spring, when the perennials need to be cut back, the shrubs lightly pruned, and the soil fertilized.

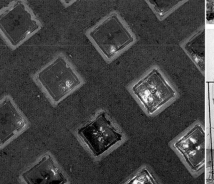

◄ OUT OF REACH

OPPOSITE PAGE This picture is taken from the end of the garden looking toward the house and really shows off the effectiveness of the raised planters against the white plastered walls. The effect is duplicated from this angle because we are looking at the top of both the shed in the foreground and the enclosure just behind it. The shed is an integral part of the stylish design of the garden, yet it is really practical and very spacious inside.

▲ WHITEWASH

TOP Under the planting troughs, in the cavity between the two exterior walls, there is sufficient space for storage and a den for Kyle, Flora's older brother. The cavity also houses hidden projectors from which, at night, images of Flora's favorite cartoon characters are beamed through holes onto the opposite wall. Flora loves mirrors, and I used them on the entrance doors to reflect light into the enclosure and double the effect of the cartoons.

▲ BENEATH YOUR FEET

ABOVE (FOUR PICTURES) A circular doorway, 6ft (1.8m) in diameter, allows access from the patio end of the enclosure and frames a view of its interior. The outdoor shower, which Flora loves to play under during the summer months, is just visible on the left.

Inside, ten concrete and glass paving slabs—originally designed to let light into English city basements—are set in a geometrical pattern into the lawn. Fiber-optic lights beneath each slab

turn the enclosure into a colorful party space at night. They were quite a job to install, but I think the effort was worth it—especially because Flora loves them so much that now they are never turned off.

Gates and railings keep Flora safe in the central area beyond the patio, which is directly outside the house. The patio's brick pavers were laid on the diagonal, the oblique lines increasing the feeling of space.

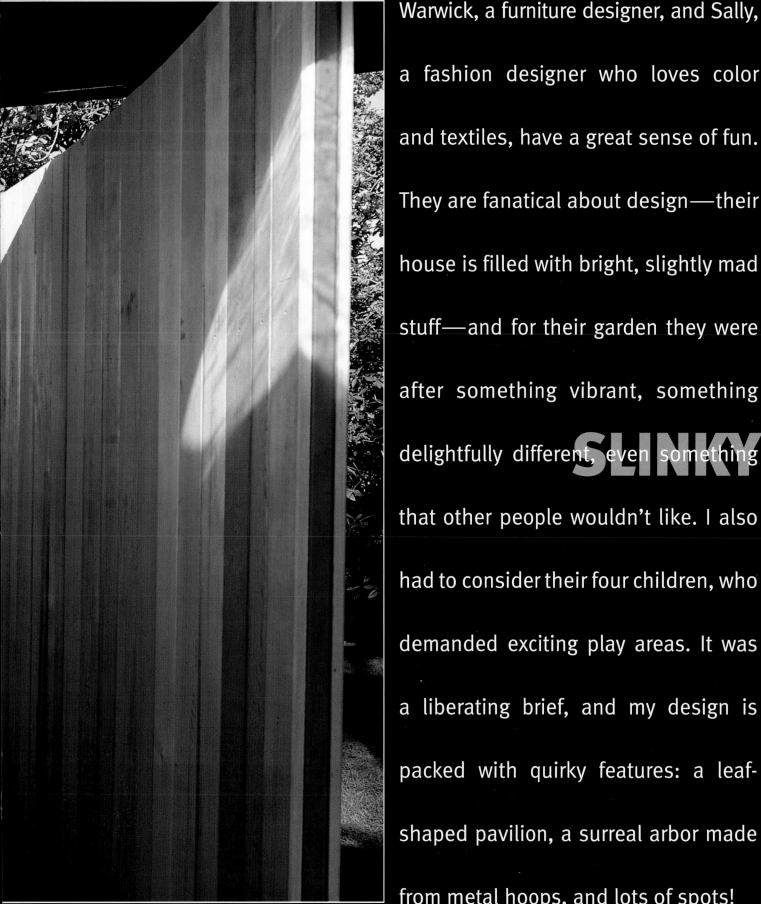

Warwick, a furniture designer, and Sally, a fashion designer who loves color and textiles, have a great sense of fun. They are fanatical about design—their house is filled with bright, slightly mad stuff—and for their garden they were after something vibrant, something delightfully different, even something **SLINKY** that other people wouldn't like. I also had to consider their four children, who demanded exciting play areas. It was a liberating brief, and my design is packed with quirky features: a leaf-shaped pavilion, a surreal arbor made from metal hoops, and lots of spots!

INSPIRATIONS

From the moment I met my clients, I knew that, for them, a contemporary garden didn't mean something minimal or stark. Going through the house and looking at Sally's work made me think of the 1950s— a golden age in British design, when modern meant forward-thinking but not frightening— when pattern, color, texture, and materials mattered.

There was something old-fashioned and family-oriented about what my clients wanted. I took inspiration from the Festival of Britain, 1950s-style furniture—notably Nelson's whimsical marshmallow sofa— and the sinuous lines of Joan Miró's surrealist paintings. Simple shapes, strong colors, and, bizarrely, spots formed the main threads of my ideas. Then, in a shop window, I glimpsed a Slinky, a sinuous metal coil toy that I thought could be made into an interesting structure to complete the design.

To divide the garden, I designed a wood and brick pavilion and set it at an angle across the center of the yard. In the area up by the house, I planned a path winding through shrubs and mature trees, while on the other side of the pavilion, I created a land of *Alice-in-Wonderland* enchantment. I planned in a curved tunnel, based on a Slinky toy, which led to the entrance of an old air-raid shelter, left over from World War II. The shelter was to be used as a playroom, and to allow light into the structure, I designed domed glass skylights in the concrete roof.

I also wanted to create a wild and colorful feature that would help to energize the garden, and came up with a fluid sculpture made up of hundreds of colored metal disks on long, flexible black rods. I planned to push these into the ground at different angles, like pins in a giant cushion, and weave the disks through the planting and around the apple trees. I imagined these spots of color looking as though someone had scattered a bag of giant M&Ms around the garden.

◄ ORIGINAL GARDEN
The garden was pretty bare—mainly lawn—but I liked the trees and wanted to retain some in the final design.

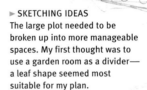

► SKETCHING IDEAS
The large plot needed to be broken up into more manageable spaces. My first thought was to use a garden room as a divider—a leaf shape seemed most suitable for my plan.

▲ SKETCHING IDEAS
The brightly colored metal disks on sticks reflect those on the pavilion and add to the retro feel of the garden. The arbor walkway reminds me of the metal Slinky toys of the 1970s.

► FINISHED DESIGN
The garden is a really exciting mix of structures and soft planting, with loads of fun features to keep the kids happy.

To make the different features in the garden look grounded, I have designed islands of plants around them and, in many cases, I've simply added to the existing mature shrubs and trees. To create contrasting colors and shapes, I used beautiful foliage plants, such as *Cotinus coggygria* Rubrifolius Group, *Euonymus japonicus*, hebes, *Pittosporum tobira*, *Prunus lusitanica*, *Skimmia japonica*, and *Viburnum davidii*. Scrambling up the arbor are climbers, such as *Trachelospermum jasminoides*, passion flowers, and ivies, which together form a tunnel of color and fragrance. And around the underground bunker, as a foil for the spotty sculpture, is a mix of grasses and sedges (*Carex oshimensis* 'Evergold', *Carex* 'Silver Sceptre', and *Miscanthus sinensis* 'Silberfeder').

PLANTS

PLANTING LIST

CLOCKWISE FROM TOP LEFT

Viburnum opulus
Vitex agnus-castus var. *latifolia*
Passiflora caerulea 'Constance Elliot'
Cotoneaster frigidus 'Cornubia'
Miscanthus sinensis 'Silberfeder'
Hedera helix 'Eva'
Cotinus coggygria Rubrifolius Group

FINAL PLAN
Although the structures are important in this garden, the plan shows how the planting creates a lush effect

COLORED DISKS
A mass "planting" of disks brightens up the area by the air-raid shelter with its glass-domed roof

SLINKY WALKWAY
A wooden path covered by a huge metal coil is a new take on the traditional arbor

PAVILION
The leaf-shaped pavilion divides the garden into two distinct areas

WOODLAND AREA
Trees from the original garden and newly planted shrubs create a woodland walk

DECKED PATIO
An area of decking leading to the woodland path sits close to the house, shaded by mature trees

This garden was all about imposing strong shapes within the rigid boundaries of a rectangular plot. I did this by creating structures such as the pavilion and "Slinky" tunnel—both of which also provide interest and entertainment. Visually, the "Slinky" creates a pull, like a time tunnel or vortex drawing you toward and then through it, keeping your eye moving forward to the end.

Built from separate metal rings, each individually bolted to steel girders beneath the wooden path, the tunnel's solid construction belies a surprising flexibility: as well as creating visual rhythm, if you run your hands along the tunnel's ribs, they begin to move in gentle waves.

The pavilion is leaf-shaped, like the lawn in the Shark Fin garden, and its crowning glory is an umbrella-like dome positioned above the skylight in the center of the roof. Made of purple disks on wires and set into a metal frame, it mirrors the spotty sculpture in the garden below. The dome can't be seen easily from the house, but as you walk toward the pavilion, you catch glimpses of it on the top, which draw you in. I think the spotty motifs are really successful in this garden, and they have led me to use spots again in more recent work.

DETAILS

◄ **CALM AND RELAXED**

OPPOSITE PAGE LEFT Earthy tones define
the pavilion. The walls are built from
warm-looking reclaimed bricks, while
the door and floorboards are cedar.
Soft brown leather chairs and foot
rests, designed and made by Warwick,
provide comfort and work well with the
elegant wooden coffee table.

◄ **FUN AND FANTASY**

OPPOSITE PAGE BELOW (THREE PICTURES)
The tunnel leads to the air-raid
shelter—now a playroom for the kids,
equipped with domed glass skylights.
   In homage to a hilarious episode
of the hit comedy *Father Ted*, the
"ever-multiplying" white rabbits were
borrowed for the day of the shoot.

▲ **FLOWING LINES**

ABOVE (TWO PICTURES) The "Slinky"
tunnel injects the design with simple
but sensuous curves. The leaf-shaped
pavilion has similar flowing lines.
   The colorful disks that decorate the
exterior walls and the domed skylight
on the roof infuse the garden with fun
and humor.

▼ **SCENE THROUGH THE SCREEN**

BELOW (THREE PICTURES) Metal disks
on sticks pushed into the ground
in large groups create a wacky *Alice-
in-Wonderland* look. In vibrant pink
blue, yellow, red, orange, and purple,
they ensure that, whatever the
season, there are spots of color
in this garden.

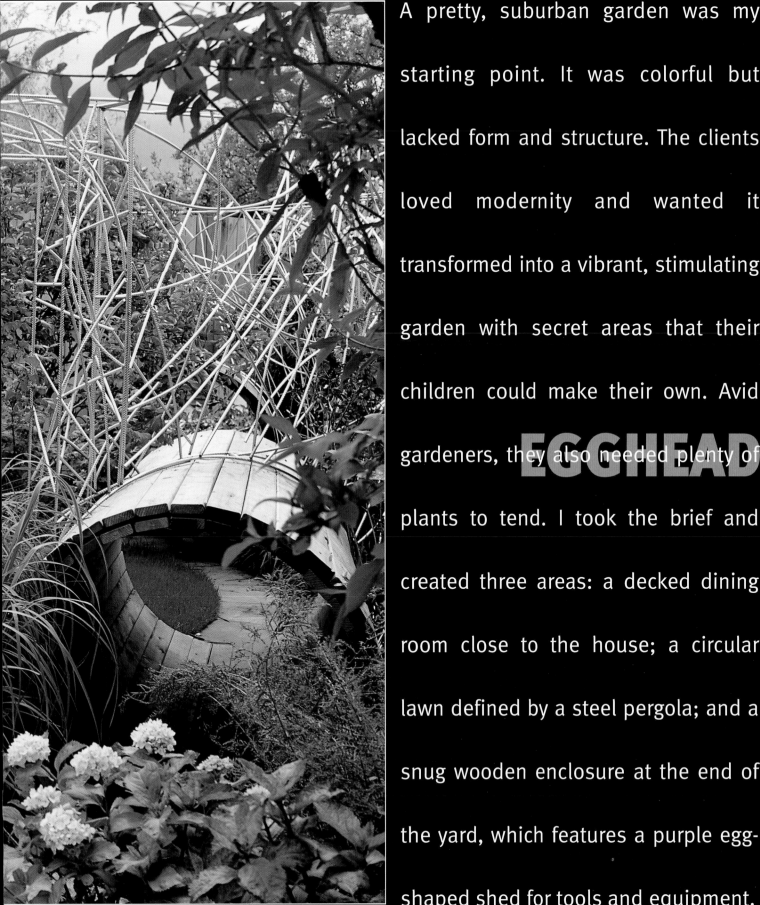

A pretty, suburban garden was my starting point. It was colorful but lacked form and structure. The clients loved modernity and wanted it transformed into a vibrant, stimulating garden with secret areas that their children could make their own. Avid gardeners, they also needed plenty of plants to tend. I took the brief and created three areas: a decked dining room close to the house; a circular lawn defined by a steel pergola; and a snug wooden enclosure at the end of the yard, which features a purple egg-shaped shed for tools and equipment.

EGGHEAD

INSPIRATIONS

My inspirations for this design were more ideas than objects: fun, shapes, color, lighting, and children playing. I wanted to create a garden that had something for everyone, a place where people could be together or alone; a series of circular rooms linked together in some way seemed fitting.

I thought of eggs, like those on the top of the Dali Museum in Spain. Their funny, slightly cartoony shape would make an intriguing shed. In my mind, I saw the egg in a curved enclosure, similar in design to a "wall of death" at a fair. Inspired by an Amnesty International sculpture I had seen in Dublin, I then came up with the idea of a wirework pergola made from stainless-steel reinforcing bars welded haphazardly together. This hard, busy structure would be a great foil for a lawn.

PLANS

My plan comprised three circular rooms: a paved courtyard next to the house, a circular lawn in the middle of the garden for the kids to play on, and, at the end of the plot, a patio encircled by curved walls made from cedar.

The couple wanted to replace a large shed, which originally stood at the back of the garden, with a smaller one. To this end, I discussed with my colleagues the plausibility of building a large, purple, egg-shaped shed. I then sketched it on my plan, creating a focal point within the cedar enclosure.

To make the garden fun for the children, I designed tunnels linking the garden rooms that would allow the little ones secret access to all areas. I also planned "invisible" doors in the enclosure walls that led to the trees at the back of the garden, where the children could create hideaways and dens. For the grownups, I designed built-in speakers to provide surround sound, and strips of blue, red, and orange lights to create a nightclub mood.

◄ SKETCHING IDEAS
I wanted to include wacky shapes in bright colors to create a sense of fun and vibrancy. A shed in the shape of an egg developed from these initial thoughts.

◄ FINISHED DESIGN
Metal, wood, and stone dominate the hard landscaping, while the garden furniture and egg-shaped shed inject color and excitement into the design.

▲ FINISHED SKETCH
The overall design had to incorporate areas for both adults and children. I decided to divide the garden into circular rooms, each with a separate feel and function.

The planting is dominated by climbers. *Actinidia kolomikta*, *Clematis* 'Alice Fisk' and *C.* 'Rouge Cardinal', *Parthenocissus henryana*, and wonderful climbing roses, such as *Rosa* 'Gloire de Dijon', scramble up the metal pergola. In the cedar enclosure, I've used a copper beech and Japanese maple as specimens in the paving, and these are accompanied by a clump of beautiful irises, some ferns, daylilies, and grasses. Mixed borders hug the decked patio and surround the pergola. In these, I have included phormiums and hostas for their architectural foliage, and *Persicaria affinis* 'Superba' and *Euonymus fortunei* 'Emerald 'n' Gold' as groundcover spilling onto the hard landscaping. The beds also offer a home for some of my favorite plants, including ligularias, with their fabulous sculptural leaves; blowzy hydrangeas; pink peonies; flat-topped achilleas; and dicentras, with their dangling heart-shaped spring flowers.

PLANTS

PLANTING LIST

CLOCKWISE FROM TOP LEFT
Euonymus fortunei 'Emerald 'n' Gold'
Parthenocissus henryana
Viburnum opulus 'Roseum'
Miscanthus sinensis 'Rotsilber'
Digitalis davisiana
Iris sibirica 'Silver Edge'
Persicaria affinis 'Superba'

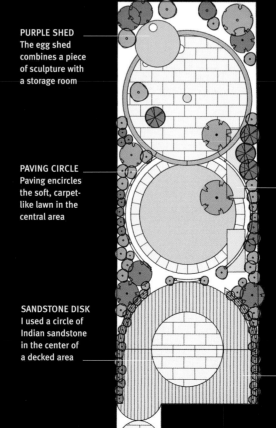

PURPLE SHED
The egg shed combines a piece of sculpture with a storage room

PAVING CIRCLE
Paving encircles the soft, carpet-like lawn in the central area

SANDSTONE DISK
I used a circle of Indian sandstone in the center of a decked area

FINAL PLAN
Seen from abov easy to see how different areas garden work to

TUNNEL LINKS
Wooden tunnels provide further elements of fun for the children

WOODEN DECK
Decking surround the stone disk and creates a great textural contrast

The egg was the centerpiece of the enclosure and a specialist bricklayer was brought in to build it. His skill was amazing, and it was a joy to see such craftsmanship. I came back one evening to check on progress, and he had just completed the brickwork—it was so brilliant that I did wonder whether we should cover it up. But in the end, I think the smooth plastered surface is more egglike and suited to my design.

The garden zings with fun and excitement, and works for both the kids and the parents. The enclosure is a relaxing and intimate space during the day, a sun trap where the family can relax, read a book, or drink coffee. But as the sun sets, the atmosphere changes and the space is transformed into a mini-nightclub. The wooden doors close to create a completely circular dance room, fitted with a stereo system and sparkling, funky lights. The cedar walls also absorb sound—helping to keep the peace with the neighbors.

DETAILS

◄ CIRCULAR ROOMS

OPPOSITE PAGE (SIX PICTURES) The circular rooms create three distinct living spaces. The terrace close to the house is large enough for a table and chairs and is used as an outdoor dining room. The circle of lawn and tunnels surrounded by the wire pergola—which up close resembles metal spaghetti—are spaces for the children to play in. The enclosure at the far end of the garden is a relaxing room for sunbathing during the day and partying at night. Here, a small fountain of water splashes onto the paving, and the egg, with its plexiglass windows and steel mirror-effect door, nestles in a corner.

▲ COLOR AND TEXTURE

ABOVE Seen from above, the different textures and colors of the three rooms are more apparent. Planting fills the gaps with more tones and textures. Climbers are just beginning to scale the steel pergola—in time, they will partially cover the frame with fragrant flowers and foliage.

► FINE DETAILS

RIGHT (FOUR PICTURES) I like the way the fine details in this garden add interest at close range. Polished strips of stainless steel and brightly colored plexiglass decorate the circular enclosure, and playful pink chairs and accessories add the final touch.

An inhospitable site, two adventurous children, and worried parents led to a back door that was kept locked. This was a real shame because the garden had great potential. Although the site sloped steeply away from the house, the view from the top was beautiful, with tree-covered hills rising on either side. But a great view doesn't solve the problems of children wanting to play and adults in need of a place to relax. My solution was three decked terraces, safely enclosed with planters, and a play area at the bottom, complete with a silver spaceship playhouse.

At the front of my mind were images of grand Italianate gardens, with terraces linked by sweeping staircases and ornate balustrades. I also remembered rice paddies in the Far East clinging to steep hillsides, with shallow pools spilling over terraces, creating dynamic architectural formations. Lookout posts, rafts, floating levels, and tree houses also seemed perfect for this site.

The molded planters were inspired by a nightclub in LA. The curved bar seemed to hover like a spaceship, and the furniture was all flowing lines. I then saw a curved desk in a local bookshop, which helped to cement my ideas.

The spaceship playhouse was dreamed up in the pub—a doodle scribbled on the back of a coaster. A *Sunday Times* magazine cover of a girl clad in a metal armor outfit inspired the metal-plate casing.

INSPIRATIONS

Working on such a steep site, I first had to assess the exact gradient and stability of the land because the engineering and manual work needed to make the garden safe would account for a large chunk of the budget.

I designed three elliptical platforms to give the garden a contemporary look, and set them at different angles. Popular in graphics and architecture, the ellipse makes its way into many of my garden designs because it's relaxed, your eye follows it around, and it provides a large surface area.

To punctuate the outer edges of the decks, I designed eggplant-colored, curved, raised planters, which would also prevent children from falling over the sides. I would have liked the fiberglass troughs to continue all the way around the decks, but the budget wouldn't allow for this, so I chose post-and-rope barriers as a compromise.

To connect the last deck with the kids' area at the bottom of the garden, I planned a fiberglass slide. Made of two sections joined together, you see them in playgrounds and swimming pools, and you can buy them from children's play equipment specialists.

◄ DURING CONSTRUCTION
The slide, which connects the third deck to the bottom of the garden, is made from two sections of molded fiberglass that have to be bolted together.

▼ SKETCHING IDEAS
To make the garden safe, I drew three oval decks stepping down the slope.

▲ MODEL GARDEN
I used the model to see how the garden would work in three dimensions, and how the decks could best be joined.

◄ FINISHED DESIGN
The decks, with their purple fiberglass planters, create layers of lush planting that cascade down the steep gradient.

PLANS

The clients are originally from the Caribbean and wante[d]

planting that reflected their homeland. Using the windo[w]

where you pack lots of plants into well-fertilized soil, I s[ow?]

purple planters with a variety of exotics, such as cannas,

cordylines, and yuccas. Mixed in with these are more trad[itional]

cottage-garden-style plants, including hellebores, hostas,

heucheras, and dicentras. The idea is that the raised plant[ers are]

easy to water and maintain, and the flower show can be ke[pt]

throughout the year by filling in any gaps with seasonal bed[ding.]

I had to design the deck around an existing maple, which [was?]

taken down for legal reasons, and this now shoots up throu[gh the]

wooden floor. I have ensured that there is a gap between the [deck]

and the trunk, to allow for growth. Elsewhere, birch trees are [planted]

into the slope to blend in with the landscape and soften the [edges.]

PLANTING LIST

CLOCKWISE FROM TOP LEFT

Alchemilla mollis
Canna 'Durban'
Pachysandra terminalis
Hosta sieboldiana
Convolvulus cneorum

FINAL PLAN
Three interconnecting
elliptical terraces
transform the hillside
into a usable space

BLUE TUBE SLIDE
A slide links the
deck to the kids'
spaceship below

SILVER ROCKET
A spaceship den
is ready for take-
off at the bottom
of the garden

MOLDED BEDS
Specially molded
purple fiberglass
planters edge
the terraces

▲ LIVING SPACE

ABOVE A once potentially dangerous slope is now a series of decked terraces. Lined with exuberant and dramatic planting, these spaces are perfect for alfresco dining, parties, or just relaxing.

◄ PLANTS ON DECKS

LEFT (TWO PICTURES) The wonderful retro-style, eggplant-colored fiberglass planters were inspired by a nightclub bar in Los Angeles. Where the land slopes steeply below the decks, the planters serve as invaluable safety barriers. The maple tree at the bottom of the garden could not be removed, so I had the lowest platform built around it.

► LIFT OFF!

OPPOSITE PAGE FROM TOP (THREE PICTURES) The denlike, silver rocket—inspired by sci-fi classics such as *Star Trek*, *Doctor Who*, and *Flash Gordon*—looks ready for takeoff. Made from strips of marine plywood, the structure is covered with squares of galvanized aluminum.

► SLIDE ON DOWN

OPPOSITE PAGE FAR RIGHT A blue tube slide links the lowest terrace with the bottom of the garden, providing the children with a fun route down. A neglected pond was filled in and the area covered with a thick, spongy layer of bark chips to give the children a soft landing when they emerge from the fiberglass slide.

This garden offered me an exciting opportunity to turn around the clients' negative feelings about their garden and to create something positive, exciting, and relaxing.

My main difficulty with the construction of the garden was making the curved containers. I knew the shape I wanted, but finding a suitable material from which to make them proved more difficult. Fiberglass, which is both flexible and strong, offered the solution.

The construction process for the planters was fascinating. I went to the supplier's workshop and outlined the deck areas on their floor. I then drew the shapes of the containers on top to finalize their measurements, and watched while my drawings became 3-D styrofoam sculptures, which were then cast in fiberglass. Almost any color and finish was available, and I enjoyed exploring ways in which this material could be used on a large scale. The resulting planting pods are relatively lightweight, which is very important, considering the loading restrictions on the elevated decks.

The clients love the garden—especially the rich colors—and the kids have great fun zipping down the slide to the spaceship.

Set in beautiful landscapes, these offices,
studios, and garden rooms offer space

INSPIRE

to reflect, to think, to create, to work

This project was about building a garden within a garden and creating an atmosphere that would stimulate the imagination. The large, three-acre site belonged to Jenny, an aspiring artist, who wanted a garden studio where she could sit and think and paint. It had to be removed from the house so that everyday worries would not interfere, and preferably close to water, with its reflective, meditative qualities. It seemed to me that a studio set on stilts above a tranquil pool would offer the perfect setting—a place to work, to be inspired, to dream.

ARTHOUSE

INSPIRATIONS

The client liked the color, vibrancy, and escapism of contemporary artists, such as Lucien Freud and Jenny Savile, and these references were at the back of my mind when creating her garden.

I love architecture from Indonesia and Bali, where buildings are constructed on stilts to protect them from the elements and other dangers. Luxurious resorts in the West are also built on stilts over lagoons— not for protection, but to create a sense of rest and tranquillity. I took these ideas and scaled them down for the studio, which I imagined floating over water. I pictured swampy plants in the pool, tall and dense, excluding the outside world. The building is inspired by beach huts and clad in corrugated iron, a material I like for its vernacular style.

I developed a plan to create a building clad in bright yellow-painted corrugated iron and supported by white oak stilts set into a large rectangular pond. The garish color was chosen to provoke reaction and to contrast with the green foliage of the existing planting. Part of one wall of the building could be lowered by means of a winch to form a pier or deck over the water, where I imagined Jenny could set up her easel and paint. The pool would reflect the ever-changing sky and clouds, the mirror effect seducing the onlooker and reinterpreting the real images. My idea was that Jenny would walk through her garden, open the doors to her studio, look out at the water, and lose herself in its reflections.

The plans didn't end there, however. I sketched in a neat lawn around the pool, inlaid with slabs of natural stone used as stepping stones. Along one side, I designed a densely planted bed, and placed white tiled walls at strategic points. These sculptural walls could at night be transformed into projector screens for Jenny's favorite works of art.

◄ ORIGINAL GARDEN
I only designed a small section of the client's large garden, which lacked focus and structure.

▲ DURING CONSTRUCTION
After the rectangular pond had been dug and planted up, we started building the arthouse and erecting white walls that at night would provide screens for projected images of paintings.

▼ FINISHED DESIGN
Painted a more subtle color, the studio would have been lost among the trees. The vivid yellow draws the eye, creating an exciting focal point.

▲ MODEL GARDEN
The rectangular studio echoes the shape of the pond and stands on stilts above the water, where it is reflected again in the surface. Part of the structure's front wall lowers to form a pier.

The planting in the pool is inspired by images of a Florida swamp. The surface of the water is punctured by cattails (*Typha latifolia*) and water lilies, the leaves of which shade the pool from the sun—which help reduce the growth of algae—and create shelter for the fish. Oxygenating plants, such as hornwort (*Ceratophyllum demersum*), help to create a sustainable ecosystem, and a few flowering aquatics, including marsh marigold (*Caltha palustris*) and *Ranunculus aquatilis*, offer color and interest.

Planting in the garden is dominated by a mixture of grasses, sedges, purple phormiums, and hypericums, together with a wonderful Indian bean tree (*Catalpa bignonioides*) that has large heart-shaped leaves and white blossom, followed, in autumn, by clusters of unusual long beans. The planting includes loads of texture and some flowers for seasonal interest, yet it needs very little maintenance.

FINAL PLAN
This design is a garden within a garden, as the plot is much larger, using borders and screens to enclose and separate it

PLANTING LIST

CLOCKWISE FROM TOP LEFT
Caltha palustris
Pistia stratiotes
Typha latifolia
Catalpa bignonioides
Ranunculus aquatilis

GARDEN POOL
The still water creates a mirror, reflecting an ever-changing skyscape

ART SCREENS
At night, works of art are projected onto these plain white screens

ARTIST'S STUDIO
A backdrop of trees frames and shelters the bright yellow studio

To complete the garden, I took inspiration from art galleries and had one of my favorite abstract paintings by the Russian artist Savtchenko copied and printed with waterproof colors onto a piece of acrylic. The painting was then mounted on a rectangular tiled wall. I wanted to show that it's not only sculpture that can be used as an installation outside—paintings can be effective, too, their colors taking on different intensities as the light changes throughout the day.

The rectangular pool brings reflections of sky and clouds into the garden. It has a mesmerizing effect, and it's easy to get lost in the mirrored surface, which seduces the viewer and reinterprets real images. Careful thought went into the design of the deck over the pool, which offers a close-up view of the water. It features a wooden shelf under the window that is hinged along the bottom edge. This folds down to create a solid surface when the wall is lowered to form the deck.

DETAILS

► **PRACTICAL CONSIDERATIONS**

ABOVE RIGHT The result is exactly what I had in mind when designing the studio. Filled with easels, canvases, brushes, and paints, it is a serious place of work—a utilitarian building inside and out. It is also equipped with running water and a large sink. The white paneled walls are insulated, which means that the studio can be used throughout the year. The walls also help to reflect light into the room.

▼ **COOL CONTRASTS**

BELOW (THREE PICTURES) The vivid yellow studio creates a startling focal point, and I wanted to ensure that the planting complemented it, rather than fought against it for attention. The smooth expanse of lawn and foliage plants cools the acid tones of the building. The green foliage offers a simple backdrop to the white-tiled projector screens, which during the day look like giant blank canvases.

► **CREATIVE COLOR**

OPPOSITE PAGE MAIN PICTURE The studio's exterior walls are clad with corrugated steel and painted bright yellow. I deliberated for some time about the color, as I knew it would be shocking, but the client supported my decision, and I'm really pleased with the result. The rectangular windows are designed to make the building resemble a modern painting: I did 40 or 50 sketches before I got the shapes right.

► **GARDEN ART**

OPPOSITE PAGE BELOW (FOUR PICTURES) I wanted to include a permanent painting in the garden, as well as transient images of artworks projected at night onto the white screens. To this end, I had a favorite abstract painting of mine copied, using waterproof paints, onto acrylic and mounted on a wall.

The paved patio is softened with small shrubs, grasses, and phormiums, and the pond is filled with cattails and reeds.

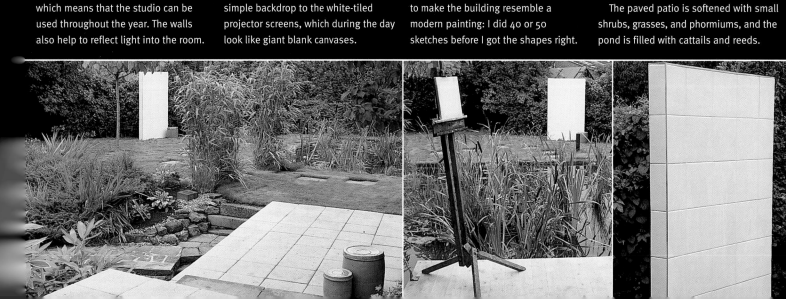

My clients, Howard and Jackie, work in advertising and have a strong sense of design. They were challenging because I knew they'd only accept what they felt was right for their garden. They wanted something quirky, but it also had to be a space that their daughter Daisy would enjoy. Their long, narrow yard was in a noisy, built-up area, and they were desperate for some peace and privacy. The top of the spaceship garden office I designed for them flips up to reveal a view of the heavens, giving the impression of wide-open spaces a million miles from the urban setting.

SPHERE

INSPIRATIONS

My clients talked to me about visiting a garden in Ireland called Liss Ard. Here they fell in love with the "sky garden"—a grass-covered amphitheater that you enter through a tunnel, lie down on the grass, and see the sky framed by a ring. They wanted to relive that experience in their own garden.

I love the natural landscape, too, and thought this was a great idea. It seemed to me that a sphere could capture the view of the sky that Jackie and Howard had described. For inspiration, I studied some of the objects in my home—an orange-shaped juicer that can be used as a pitcher when you take the top off, and a radio with a slice taken off the front that forms the face. I also love those 1970s "space helmet" TVs, and spherical chairs that hang from the ceiling.

I was also swayed by Jackie's love of pink—she and Daisy dressed in it every day.

Combining my inspirations, I started to sketch an office in the shape of a silver orb, clad with bands of polished stainless steel. Inside, the sphere was decorated with tiny circular ceramic tiles. To free up floor space, I designed a wall-mounted bench that clung to the circumference.

I then designed little flaps all over the structure that could be opened to reveal rectangles of colored glass. When the sphere was lit from inside at night, these colorful windows would transform it into a giant lantern. To add to the effect, I experimented with ways in which the top could be winched open to reveal uninterrupted views of the sky. The bottom of the garden was the perfect landing site for my sphere, and I planned a stepping-stone pathway leading to its door.

Two metal spherical seats mirror the shape of the office: on my plan I sketched a small one for Jackie, close to the house, and a larger one for Howard, halfway down the garden. Suspended from metal tripods, I showed them twisting and turning over flower beds.

The couple enjoys entertaining friends, so I included a small patio in a sunny spot outside the kitchen door.

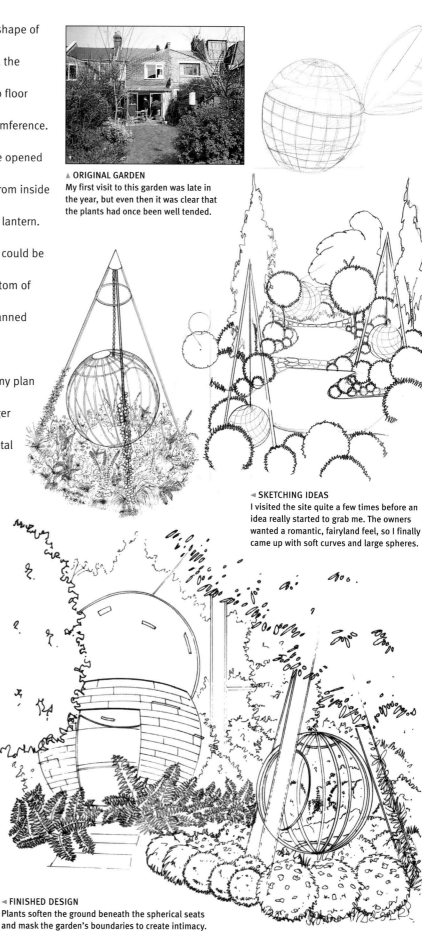

▲ ORIGINAL GARDEN
My first visit to this garden was late in the year, but even then it was clear that the plants had once been well tended.

◄ SKETCHING IDEAS
I visited the site quite a few times before an idea really started to grab me. The owners wanted a romantic, fairyland feel, so I finally came up with soft curves and large spheres.

◄ FINISHED DESIGN
Plants soften the ground beneath the spherical seats and mask the garden's boundaries to create intimacy.

PLANTING LIST

CLOCKWISE FROM TOP LEFT

Campanula glomerata 'Superba'
Digitalis grandiflora
Spiraea japonica 'Little Princess'
Geranium x *oxonianum* 'Claridge Druce'
Lavandula angustifolia
Nothofagus antarctica
Humulus lupulus 'Aureus'

The original garden was full of plants, and I retained many of them to provide a rich tapestry of foliage. However, I did add to the planting, and have used ferns, including *Polypodium vulgare*, and trees, including liquidambar, *Nothofagus antarctica*, and *Acacia dealbata*, along the boundaries. The trees and lush plants help to transform the site into an enclosed magical landscape. A hidden, secret area behind the sphere is planted with native plants, including birches, hazels, and foxgloves. The tripods supporting the seats are entwined with golden hop (*Humulus lupulus* 'Aureus') and *Trachelospermum jasminoides*. And as a nod to Jackie's love of pink, the dazzling *Rosa* Wiltshire is planted *en masse* beside the house.

FINAL PLAN
This romantic, fairytale plot is dotted with spheres and traversed by a winding path

SPHERICAL OFFICE
The shiny, spherical office looks like a futuristic spaceship that has crashed into a prehistoric landscape of tree ferns

STEPPING-STONE PATH
The path leads visitors down the length of the garden through the lush plants and trees toward the silver office

GLOBE CHAIRS
This is one of two giant spherical chairs in the garden. Made from steel, they are suspended from tall, metal tripods

EXISTING PLANT LIFE
Some of the garden's existing planting has been retained, giving the garden a mature look and shielding it from neighboring properties

The spherical steel office transforms this garden from a leafy suburban yard into something out of the ordinary. Designed to surprise and delight, you chance upon the sphere nestling among the ferns, as though you've woken, bleary-eyed, to find that last night's dream was true and aliens really have landed in your back yard.

The shiny steel surface is vibrant year-round, reflecting scudding clouds, rain, sun, and snow, but always remaining light and bright, its little windows winking and beckoning you to take a second look. Its function as an office, though, makes it more than a trivial piece of garden sculpture. For me this is vital—if garden structures are to stand the test of time, they should always have a practical use. Likewise, the spherical seats have a graphic quality, mirroring the shape of the office, yet they offer comfort—especially when lined with a quilt— and a 360-degree view of the garden as they slowly revolve.

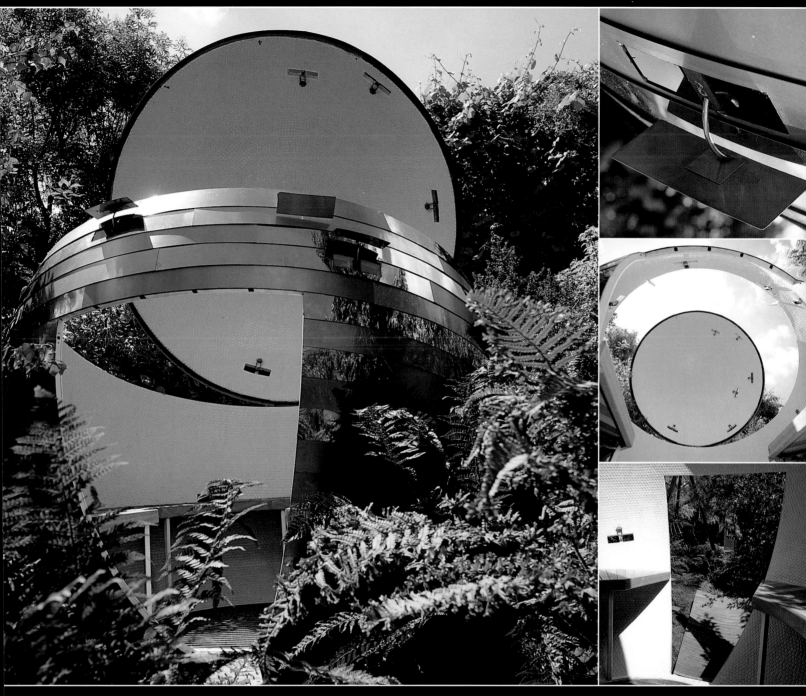

◄ METAL RIBS

OPPOSITE PAGE FAR LEFT The garden's metal-ribbed, spherical seats were inspired by 1960s acrylic seating. Suspended from sturdy tripods on heavy-duty chains, they twist and turn to reveal different views of the garden. At night, lit from below, they are transformed into giant cages of light.

Both the spherical seats and the office were built off-site and had to be lifted by crane over the house and into the back garden.

◄ PARTY PIECE

OPPOSITE PAGE LEFT (EIGHT PICTURES) Beautiful foliage trees, like this robinia, are mirrored in the shiny surface of the office. Adding further to the drama in the garden, as the seats revolve, they cast delicate shadows on the grassy floor.

The steel office also makes a great party room. The doorway lowers like a drawbridge, reminiscent of alien spacecraft in early sci-fi films. The roof also opens up, lifted by a mechanical winch, to reveal ever-changing skies.

▲ ALIENS HAVE LANDED

ABOVE Set into a slight depression and surrounded by lush green ferns, the garden's architectural focal point looks like a futuristic spaceship that has crash-landed into *Jurassic Park*. The wacky flip-up lid is a fun feature and also fulfills the clients' request to see the sky. Inspired by the skies they saw on a trip to Ireland, the couple realized that the only way to achieve views of vast open spaces from their small urban plot would be to look up!

▲ LIGHTING UP

ABOVE (THREE PICTURES) Small flaps push open from inside the office to reveal windows of colored glass. At night, these are illuminated, adding to the spaceship illusion.

The view from the office shows how the planting in the rest of the garden works to soften the hard structures. Most of the mature trees were in the garden when I first saw it, and I wanted to retain their leafy canopies in the final design.

When I first visited this garden, I found a beautiful range of plants and a sensible design already in place. But the clients were looking for something new—a contemporary design, but not overpowering in a harsh way. They wanted a family garden where their two daughters and dog could play, and where they could entertain. Passionate about plants, they also asked that I include the cottage-style planting that they love. The garden room injects an element of modernity and acts as a backdrop to my design, while the fountain offers sound and movement.

THE OVAL

INSPIRATIONS

The oval lawn, planting, and paving came to me without any trouble, but the garden building presented a problem. I began by thinking about a long barrel lying on its side, but it wasn't right for the site. Then, while driving home in a rented car, I looked down at the instrument display panel. The shape was fantastic—long, deep, and curved. It reminded me of London's NatWest Media Centre, built by Future Systems, and I knew this was the shape I'd been looking for.

A while later, I saw a preview for an exhibition by the Korean artist Do-Ho Suh that featured a metal tunic constructed from thousands of dogtags. Beautifully formed, it flowed down to spill onto the floor in a wonderful swirl. I loved the idea of a solid material flowing over my chosen lines, so I created a curved building with a metal frame covered in linking squares of stainless steel.

I designed the podlike building to fit in with the existing garden scheme and sketched it on my plan nestling under a mature pear tree. I devised a pneumatically operated door for the front that would lift up to create a sort of canopy — making the building look a bit like a spaceship. And after a lot of discussions with Sean Cunningham, my project manager, and Tom Gallagher and Ryan Tautari from Elite Metalcraft, I changed my mind about the stainless-steel roof cladding and opted instead for copper. Work began on the pod before my plan was finished. Its steel frame was very impressive and inspired me to replicate the design for a large pergola at the opposite end of the garden. This second feature would echo the internal structure of the building and create a dramatic entrance to the garden.

Planting was intrinsic to the success of my plan, and I packed all available spaces around the edge of the garden with shrubs, trees, and flowering herbaceous plants.

◄ ORIGINAL GARDEN
Already nicely planted, this garden was also well maintained, and we agreed that an existing pear tree, a pieris, and a Japanese maple should be retained in the final design.

▼ SKETCHING IDEAS
My sketches reflect the symmetry and curved lines that appealed to my clients.

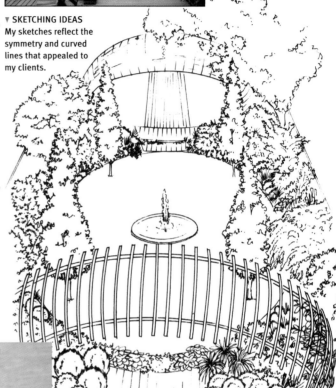

► MODEL GARDEN
A massive metal frame, which we dubbed "the eyelashes," forms the main support for the garden building.

▼ DURING CONSTRUCTION
The metal frame was covered with a copper roof, which, when exposed to the elements, will eventually turn gray-green. Inside the building, the frame has been left uncovered and forms a wonderful vaulted roof.

► FINISHED DESIGN
A second metal frame, echoing the main covered structure, makes a perfect pergola for the entrance to the garden.

PLANS

It was obvious that my clients loved their plants, so I made sure that many already existing in their garden were retained in my design. There was a wonderful pear tree, a tall pieris, and an acer planted to celebrate the birth of one of their daughters. There was also a lovely laburnum in a neighboring plot which, with some careful planning, now looks as though it emerges from my client's garden. To these, I added four beautiful hornbeams toward the boundaries of the oval lawn— I hoped these would create a feeling of enclosure by keeping the focus in the garden rather than encouraging people to look outside. The borders are filled with lavender, hostas, nepeta, hydrangeas, geraniums, roses, peonies, and rosemary, providing masses of flowers and scent. The arbour is planted with *Humulus lupulus* 'Aureus', wisteria, and actinidia, which will, in time, clothe it with foliage and flowers.

PLANTING LIST

CLOCKWISE FROM TOP LEFT

Trollius x *cultorum* 'Orange Princess'
Paeonia lactiflora 'Sarah Bernhardt'
Lavandula dentata
Geranium himalayense 'Gravetye'
Rosa rugosa
Nepeta 'Six Hills Giant'
Hosta 'So Sweet'

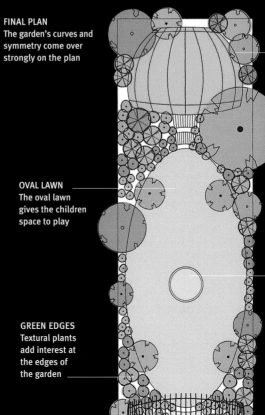

FINAL PLAN
The garden's curves and symmetry come over strongly on the plan

VERDIGRIS
The copper roof of the garden room will eventually turn gray-green

OVAL LAWN
The oval lawn gives the children space to play

SAFETY ASPECTS
A removable grille over the fountain keeps young children safe

GREEN EDGES
Textural plants add interest at the edges of the garden

METAL EYELASHES
The pergola at the garden's entrance echoes the interior

My clients Will and Denise absolutely love the garden, and when I returned a year or so after it was finished, I was pleased to see that the Jekyll-style cottage-garden planting had matured really well.

In terms of both the carpentry and the metalwork, this garden is pure craftsmanship—but there were some pretty hairy moments during its construction. We work to a fixed time scale on TV projects, and the night before this one had to be completed, the team was in a state of pure panic. We were having trouble getting the weighted pneumatic door to work properly, and at about four o'clock in the morning we decided to send it back to the factory. It was trial and error, but we got there in the end, and it's still working today.

The room is set below ground level, which meant we had to consider the water table. To prevent flooding, a submerged pump was installed to remove any surface water before it can get into the building.

◀ SOFTENING THE EDGES

OPPOSITE PAGE LEFT I have combined a semi-formal design with symmetrical beds and a central fountain with more radical elements, such as the steel-girder pergola. The pergola's hard lines offer a dramatic contrast to the soft, flowering perennials below.

▲ THE FLICK OF A SWITCH

ABOVE (FOUR PICTURES) Raised and lowered pneumatically at the flick of a switch, the garden room's cat-flap-like wood and steel door also serves as a shelter over the deck outside. The curved glass windows on either side of the door offer a view out across the garden to the house.

I chose copper for the roof of the building because I love the way it evolves over time, changing color as it reacts with the atmosphere, and taking on the soft gray-green tints of verdigris. The planting is a mix of herbaceous perennials and dramatic trees and shrubs, including this Japanese acer

► LONG, BLACK LASHES

RIGHT The metal frame, which forms the internal skeleton of the garden room, was covered with wood and clad in copper. But it seemed a shame to cover up this beautiful piece of work, so I commissioned a second and used it as a pergola at the other end of the garden (see main picture opposite). Standing just outside the house, the pergola frames the garden beyond and replicates the curves of the garden room, unifying the design. When sitting on the deck under the pergola, you get a view of the supporting skeleton inside the room, which, from this perspective, resembles a huge eye with long, black lashes.

The fountain is a bubbling focal point in the middle of the oval lawn and spills over into a small pond. Since children would be playing in this area, safety was an issue, so I designed a sturdy steel grille that can be slotted over the open water

My clients wanted something new and different, but they didn't know what. They had no specific reference points but were avid readers of style magazines, which gave me some clues as to what they would like. Their rectangular plot was a blank canvas, apart from some shrubs hugging the boundaries, and needed an innovative design to make it challenging, usable, and exciting. I decided to break up the site into compartments, but instead of using traditional materials or hedging to carve it up, I created sharp-edged tunnels made from hard, urban steel.

STEEL TUNNELS

INSPIRATIONS

I love the idea of surprises in a garden, of leading people from A to B but not letting them see what's in front of them, building up a sense of anticipation, as in a maze or secret pathway.

Walking through tunnels and subways gave me another idea. The simple tunnel device has been used for centuries by designers, but I knew that in this garden my tunnels had to be made of steel to give them an edgy, contemporary look.

When I visited a foundry, I saw how steel could be infinitely malleable, and rolled, pressed, hammered, or cut into almost any shape. It's a material I love to work with, and while watching reruns of the cult TV show *Doctor Who*, I realized it's because for me steel conjures up images of space travel and brave new worlds.

I also like the way it reacts with the elements, oxidizing and developing a wonderful orange-brown patina.

PLANS

The house is raised 5ft (1.5m) above the garden, which meant that you could stand on the back step and take in the whole site in just one glance. I knew that by dividing the area into compartments, using steel tunnels set on diagonals across the plot, I could create mystery by ensuring that no two parts of the garden could be seen at one time. Between the tunnels, I designed garden rooms: a patio area close to the house set on three levels; a pool and terrace for relaxing and looking at the plants; and a vegetable garden at the back of the plot where the clients could grow their own produce. The tunnels would make wonderful backdrops for each space, as well as providing exciting walkways through the garden.

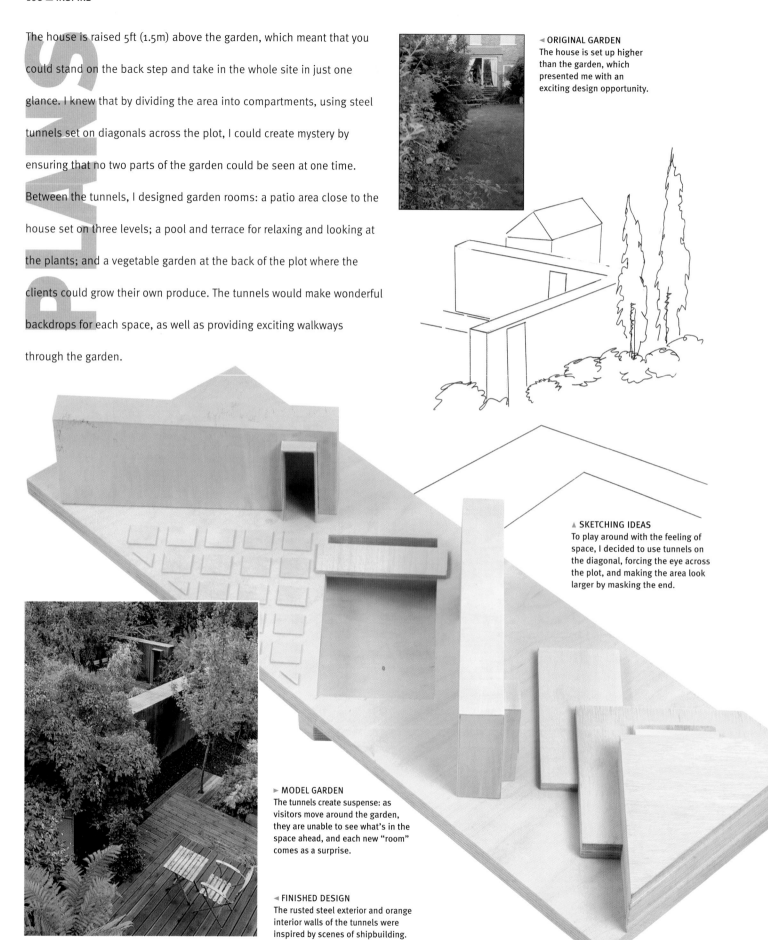

◄ ORIGINAL GARDEN
The house is set up higher than the garden, which presented me with an exciting design opportunity.

▲ SKETCHING IDEAS
To play around with the feeling of space, I decided to use tunnels on the diagonal, forcing the eye across the plot, and making the area look larger by masking the end.

► MODEL GARDEN
The tunnels create suspense: as visitors move around the garden, they are unable to see what's in the space ahead, and each new "room" comes as a surprise.

◄ FINISHED DESIGN
The rusted steel exterior and orange interior walls of the tunnels were inspired by scenes of shipbuilding.

This was a challenging project in terms of planting because the clients wanted different things from the garden. The husband was a traditionalist, while his wife was open to new ideas. To satisfy him, there is a vegetable garden at the very back of the garden, and in the beds close to the deck, directly outside the house, I have left the ferns and liriopes that were already growing there.

Planting in the rest of the garden is more experimental. The sunken pool behind the first tunnel is filled with irises and water lilies. And the metal bridge, edged with a clump of bamboo, leads to a small paved courtyard crisscrossed with turf. I planted a border alongside the second tunnel with strappy-leaved daylilies (*Hemerocallis*) and ornamental grasses, such as pampas grass (*Cortaderia selloana*) and zebra grass (*Miscanthus sinensis* 'Zebrinus').

PLANTING LIST

CLOCKWISE FROM TOP LEFT
Hemerocallis lilioasphodelus
Phyllostachys
Euonymus fortunei 'Emerald Gaiety'
Robinia pseudoacacia 'Frisia'
Cortaderia selloana
Liriope muscari
Kitchen garden

FINAL PLAN
Metal tunnels placed on the diagonal create three main garden "rooms"

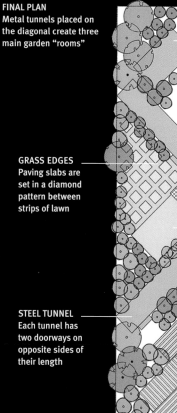

GREENHOUSE
The final tunnel leads visitors into the kitchen garden area

GRASS EDGES
Paving slabs are set in a diamond pattern between strips of lawn

SHALLOW POND
A metal grille acts as a bridge across this shallow pond

STEEL TUNNEL
Each tunnel has two doorways on opposite sides of their length

STRIPED DECKS
Square decks are laid diagonally, creating a sense of movement

PLANTS

The tunnel dividers create a wonderful air of secrecy that pervades the whole garden. As well as being functional walkways, I see the tunnels as modern sculptures, or a piece of installation art—especially when the sun hits the burnt orange interior walls, and highlights the plate-steel exterior, which takes on a beautiful rust color as it oxidizes.

Walking through a tunnel is like entering a maze, except that you don't get lost, because they are enclosed and the openings to the side are almost hidden from view. Sun streams through these doorways, creating a sense of anticipation—light at the end of the tunnel—and you emerge from the gloom into an unknown area, feeling slightly disoriented. At night, the tunnels are lit, giving the garden a psychedelic feel.

The garden rooms enclosed by the house and tunnels are distinctive in form and function. The patio consists of blocks of decking set on three levels, each at an angle of 45 degrees to the back of the house. Sandwiched between the first and second tunnels is a private patio garden, and in an open sunny site at the end of the plot, there is a kitchen garden, crammed with fruit and vegetables.

DETAILS

▲ SECRET GARDENS

ABOVE One of the best ways to view this garden is from an upstairs window. From here the individual "garden rooms" can be seen as a whole. The idea of garden rooms isn't a new one, but on this project I've given it a modern twist. The steel and wood geometric structures have a contemporary look and are unlike anything I have ever seen before in a garden design.

◄ LEVEL BEST

LEFT (TWO PICTURES) To create greater interest in the area just outside the house, wooden decking has been built on three levels linked by steps.

In the middle garden by the pond, stone paving slabs are interspersed with strips of sod.

► LIGHT FANTASTIC

OPPOSITE PAGE (SEVEN PICTURES) Hard-landscaping materials in this part of the garden include wood, rusted sheet steel, and stone, which work together to create an earthy, natural-looking effect.

At night the tunnels are lit from inside and emit a yellow glow from the openings. And the graphic contrast between the warm orange interior walls and the shiny steel walkways is simply beautiful.

Tall grasses squeezed into a narrow bed between the tunnels and pool bring the harsh, inorganic surfaces to life. Where the materials used are hard and uncompromising, plants play a crucial role in softening the scene and preventing the design from looking rigid and stark.

Whether your jello comes with ice cream or laced with vodka, these gardens are for sharing **PARTY** with friends and kicking off your shoes

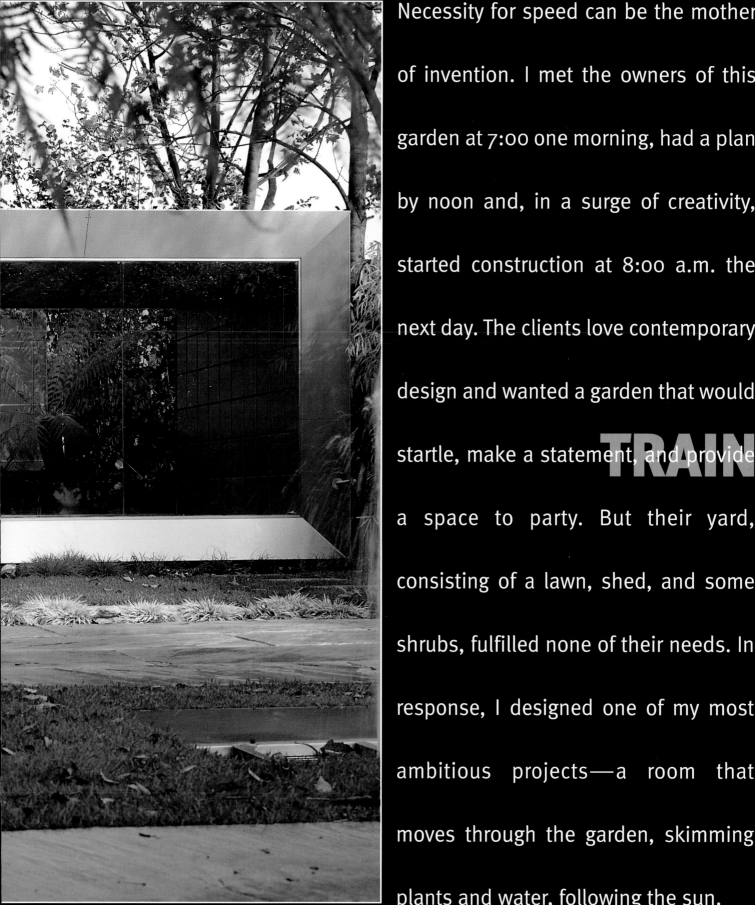

Necessity for speed can be the mother of invention. I met the owners of this garden at 7:00 one morning, had a plan by noon and, in a surge of creativity, started construction at 8:00 a.m. the next day. The clients love contemporary design and wanted a garden that would startle, make a statement, and provide a space to party. But their yard, consisting of a lawn, shed, and some shrubs, fulfilled none of their needs. In response, I designed one of my most ambitious projects—a room that moves through the garden, skimming plants and water, following the sun.

TRAIN

This wide, open plot offered me the opportunity to develop the concept of movement in the garden—not the movement of nature, but of transportation systems. I have always wanted to build a garden that could move in some way—perhaps on a conveyor belt, or on tracks like a train or tram. My colleague Sean Cunningham, who loves and understands cars, helped to devise the mechanics that would allow us to build a moving pavilion for this garden. To show him the sort of thing I was after, I played him a Jamiroquai video in which Jay Kay dances in a room with a moving floor and furniture.

I looked at Le Corbusier's Villa Savoye, built in a Paris suburb in 1929, for the shape and form of my traveling pavilion. And the planting plan was inspired by Mondrian paintings, with their bold, geometric shapes, and also the gridlike *Top of the Pops* logo.

INSPIRATIONS

PLANS

Standing in my clients' garden early that first morning, I immediately had the idea of building a pavilion. The building would function as a space to eat, drink, and relax in, and would also frame a view. I designed a long and wide, low-slung, rectangular structure that could travel the length of the garden on tracks. As it moved, appearing to float effortlessly above grid-shaped beds, it would play with perspective in a physical way. The pavilion could also be parked at any point along its trackway, and three stop-off points made from paving and decking would provide safe, dry surfaces for "passengers" to alight. Stepping stones set in a straight line 10ft (3m) from the right-hand perimeter would link the alighting points. I sketched in jets of water in front of the pavilion—as it approached, the jets would be detected by sensors and turn off automatically as the structure passed over. I also designed a giant lightbox within the line of vision of the pavilion, which echoed its shape and would provide a tall, vertical accent.

► SKETCHING IDEAS
My first idea was a long, rectangular pavilion—a shape I often use because it sits well within the suburban vernacular. I wanted it to slide back and forth on tracks through the garden.

► MODEL GARDEN
The large, orange lightbox that stands upright at the back of the garden appears to get smaller as the pavilion rolls away from it.

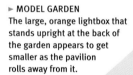

▼ FINISHED DESIGN
Sleek and simple, the stainless-steel-clad pavilion shimmers and shines in the sun as it glides across the plot.

Along the sides of the garden I used bamboos, such as *Phyllostachys* and *Fargesia*, which rustle as the stainless-steel-clad building brushes past. Wonderfully architectural, the stems and foliage of these bamboos surround the garden in shades of green and gold. Planted between them is *Euphorbia characias*, another structural plant, which has stiff blue-green fingerlike foliage and eyecatching lime green flowerheads in late spring.

Low-growing plants that won't be damaged as the pavilion passes over them are set in rectangular gridlike blocks in the center of the garden. I chose these mainly for their texture and leaf shape. The huge shiny leaves of *Bergenia* 'Sunningdale', for instance, contrast superbly with the spiky needles of *Juniperus rigida* subsp. *conferta* and frothy *Waldsteinia ternata*. In places the planting is interspersed with gravel and brightly colored paving slabs laid out in geometric shapes.

PLANTING LIST

CLOCKWISE FROM TOP LEFT

Bergenia 'Sunningdale'
Fargesia nitida
Liriope muscari 'Royal Purple'
Waldsteinia ternata
Phyllostachys aureosulcata f. *spectabilis*
Juniperus rigida subsp. *conferta*
Acorus gramineus

PLANTS

FINAL PLAN
I love the idea of garden structures that move. This pavilion slides on tracks from one end of the plot to the other

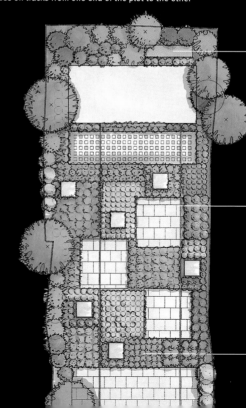

LIGHTBOX
The orange screen appears to change size as the pavilion moves to and fro

LANDING PADS
Three patios form safe entry and exit points for passengers

LOW-RISE PLANT
Ground-hugging plants allow the pavilion to pass over them

The mechanics of the moving pavilion are pretty advanced. Safety was an issue that had to be addressed—such a large structure moving on tracks through a garden is potentially lethal. The pavilion is controlled by a switch inside the structure that you have to keep pressed down until the building reaches your chosen spot. Boxes welded to the front and back of the pavilion transmit a sensor beam, which if broken by a person or animal will cause the building to stop immediately. The sensor is very sophisticated and is also linked to the fountains that dot the garden—when the beam detects the upward spray of a fountain, the pavilion continues to move but the water is cut off temporarily until it has passed overhead.

This is a prototype garden, a truly contemporary garden, that utilizes modern technology to its limits. I love it because it's wacky and different from anything I've seen before.

◄ ON THE MOVE

OPPOSITE PAGE (TWO PICTURES) The pavilion stretches almost to the full width of the garden. Spacious and light inside, it is a great room for entertaining.

As a piece of design, the building works on a number of levels: the steel frame outlines the café-style interior and the view of the back of the garden, while the glass walls ensure that, even when parked close to the house, the pavilion never looks oppressive or heavy. Simple modern furniture completes the light, clean design. On a practical note, the only drawback is that to preserve the sleek look, the owners have to keep the interior clear of clutter.

▲ GARDEN VIEWS

ABOVE (FOUR PICTURES) Stark and modern, I think the pavilion works in this garden setting because it provides an exciting contrast to the leafy perimeters. And from inside, the sunny space offers an all-around view of the garden.

The orange screen, which is illuminated at night, mirrors the shape of the pavilion and injects color and a vertical dimension into the design.

► FOUNTAINS

RIGHT (TWO PICTURES) Because the plants beside the tracks had to be low and almost one-dimensional, I introduced movement and height with a series of tall fountains.

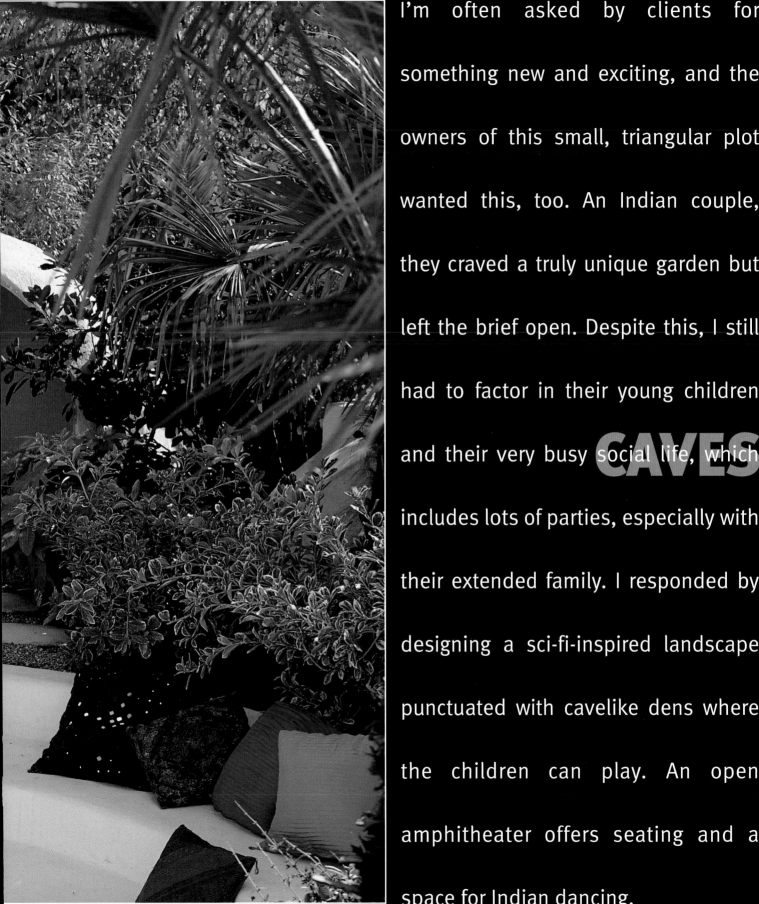

I'm often asked by clients for something new and exciting, and the owners of this small, triangular plot wanted this, too. An Indian couple, they craved a truly unique garden but left the brief open. Despite this, I still had to factor in their young children and their very busy social life, which includes lots of parties, especially with their extended family. I responded by designing a sci-fi-inspired landscape punctuated with cavelike dens where the children can play. An open amphitheater offers seating and a space for Indian dancing.

CAVES

INSPIRATIONS

The overall look of this garden is inspired by the 1960s sci-fi movies I used to watch as a child. Set in futuristic places, they had fantastic landscapes full of prehistoric-looking plants.

I also love the work of Japanese architects Ushida-Findlay, whose Truss Wall House in Tokyo, with its balloon tile courtyard, sets aside the rules.

I wanted cavelike enclosures in my futuristic landscape, like the Cappadocia Caves in Turkey, or the igloo on top of a pint of Guinness Extra Cold, which I saw on an ad. I struggled with the exact design of the caves for a long while. Then, an intriguing house on the Côte d'Azur caught my eye in the magazine *Architectural Digest*. It looked like something from a Bond movie. And a week later I was jumping excitedly over its domed roofs, my ideas crystallizing as I hopped from one form to another.

The site itself was inhospitable, not in terms of access or aspect, just in terms of shape: it was a triangle that came to an end at an awkward point. It had also been neglected for many years. The first thing I needed to do was to think of a design that would draw the eye away from the boundaries. Gathering spaces were also required, including dens for the whole family, and stimulating play areas for the children.

I designed three main structures in the garden: a walk-through cave with large openings on both sides that would act as a shelter and a "landscape framer"; an enclosed cave at the end of the garden with a white crumb-rubber floor—the texture is so lovely that guests wouldn't need other seating; and, finally, an igloo, which was inspired by Inuit dwellings. Only accessible by smaller children, it would provide the perfect hiding place. The sunken mini-amphitheater was positioned close to the house to act as a meeting, seating, and dancing area. Instead of a path, I designed stepping stones made from irregular blobs of white concrete, which would draw the eye down the garden.

▼ FINISHED GARDEN
Round stepping stones lead through the garden, echoing the domed roofs and curved doorways of the caves.

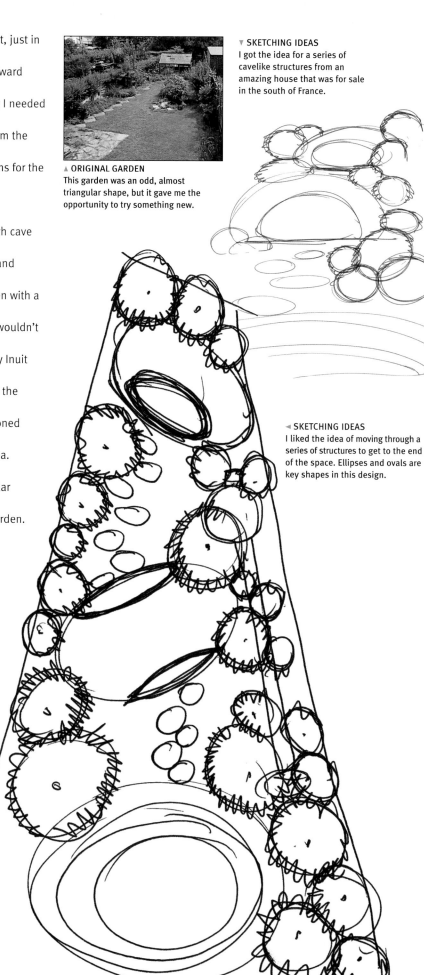

▲ ORIGINAL GARDEN
This garden was an odd, almost triangular shape, but it gave me the opportunity to try something new.

▼ SKETCHING IDEAS
I got the idea for a series of cavelike structures from an amazing house that was for sale in the south of France.

◄ SKETCHING IDEAS
I liked the idea of moving through a series of structures to get to the end of the space. Ellipses and ovals are key shapes in this design.

The planting style relies on eucalyptus, *Miscanthus sinensis*, *Trachycarpus fortunei*, various sorts of euonymus, and the tree fern *Dicksonia squarrosa*, to create a tropical ambience. This particular tree fern is especially wonderful with its dramatic, dark, almost jet black trunk. However, it is not as hardy as some other tree ferns and will only survive in mild climates. Cannas inject tropical color into the planting from summer until the first frosts. These, too, may need protection during the winter. The flat heads of sedum flowers create spots of pink along the walkways and attract butterflies. Of all the varieties of sedum, 'Brilliant' seems to be their favorite. And the vertical spires of purple liatris contrast with the horizontal lines of the amphitheater.

PLANTS

PLANTING LIST

CLOCKWISE FROM TOP LEFT
Canna 'Assaut'
Euonymus fortunei
Euonymus alatus
Sedum spectabile 'Brilliant'
Trachycarpus fortunei
Liatris spicata
Peeling bark of *Eucalyptus parvifolia*

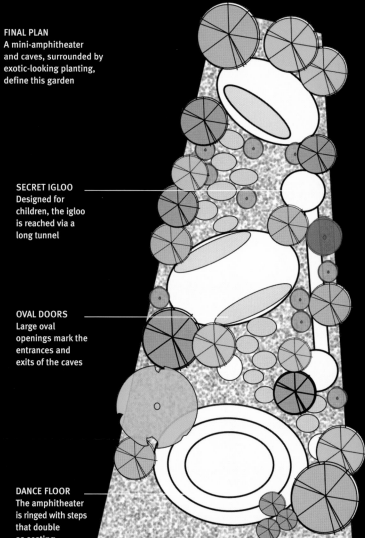

FINAL PLAN
A mini-amphitheater and caves, surrounded by exotic-looking planting, define this garden

SECRET IGLOO
Designed for children, the igloo is reached via a long tunnel

OVAL DOORS
Large oval openings mark the entrances and exits of the caves

DANCE FLOOR
The amphitheater is ringed with steps that double as seating

DETAILS

Curved rooms are fantastic forms for the human body; they seem to create a sense of security, and their exterior appearance belies the sense of space they offer inside. Entering these structures can be both a soothing and an exciting experience, especially, as in this garden, when they are surrounded by a miniature exotic jungle. To screen the neighboring properties and draw the eye inward, I have used very basic design techniques, such as planting tall trees and climbers along the boundaries and within the garden, which has allowed me to create a space that's independent of its surroundings.

This was a difficult garden, both physically and intellectually. I had to come to terms with the idea of creating such a permanent structure in a relatively small space, and in a suburban setting. The garden also relates to nothing I have ever seen before, and it was brave of the clients to commission it. Their enjoyment is the true reward.

▲ FRAMING VIEWS

ABOVE There are three cavelike structures in the garden. This one, in the center of the yard, is a walk-through, open-sided construction that offers some shelter. As well as acting as a focal point, both openings are designed to frame the views on either side.

◄ SECRET HIDEY-HOLE

LEFT The second enclosure is a great hideaway for both parents and children. It has just one entrance and a crumb-rubber floor, which is both warm to touch and waterproof. Once inside, the surrounding tree ferns, grasses, and shrubs screen you from the outside world, making this a secret space. I have used a limited palette of plants, most of which were chosen for their architectural qualities and their ability to provide textural and color relief from the concrete structures.

Just visible on the left is one of the round concrete containers filled with water, reflecting plants and sky.

► MINI-AMPHITHEATER

OPPOSITE PAGE (FOUR PICTURES) The mini-amphitheater is just outside the back door, making access to it easy for party guests. A great space for dancing and watching the action, the cool white benches can be livened up and made more comfortable with colorful Indian silk cushions. Small lights are also dotted around the dance floor. The caves are party places, too, where people who want to relax and talk can escape from the music and dancing.

The last cave is more like an igloo, and is a fun place for the children to play. Smaller than the caves, it is accessed through a large concrete tube. On an aesthetic level, I like the irony of a structure that was originally designed for harsh, snowy landscapes crash-landing among lush, tropical plants—the stuff of sci-fi movies, but it's actually taking place in a suburban garden. Amazingly, the igloo seems to fit perfectly into this green environment.

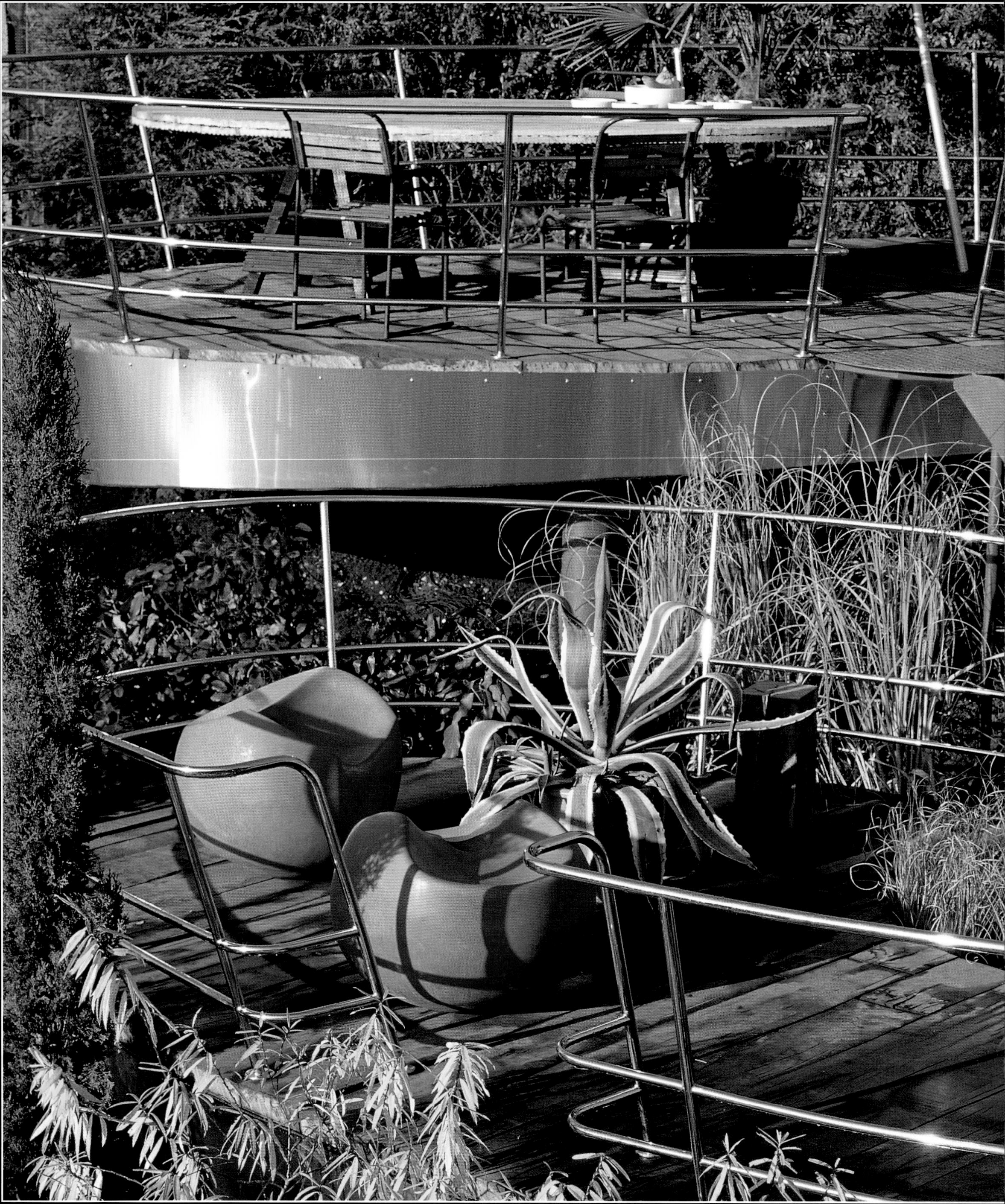

Extreme gardening is an interesting concept—you're always guided by your site and the conditions it offers. Faced with this steeply sloping plot, running up and away from the house, my limitations were obvious. I could either go with the topography, or try to tame it. The clients have a young family and needed a recreation area, but had no ambitions to be mountaineers, so the only option was to tame it. My design has flat surfaces on different levels where adults can relax and kids can play. A practical, visually exciting garden, it is also easy to maintain.

HOVERCRAFT

INSPIRATIONS

Floating, a favorite theme of mine, is what this garden is all about. I love the idea of heavy objects defying gravity, allowing you to ride on top of them. This garden, to me, also needed a sense of momentum, pushing you up and up to the top. I thought of pods that seemed to float above the ground, like the spaceships in those old sci-fi movies of the '50s and '60s.

Another reference point for this garden was the Oklahoma State Bank—a fantastic building with roofs that look like flying saucers.

Crafts full of people hovering above land and sea is another slightly surreal image that I've integrated into the design. And massive oil rigs straddling the ocean, with legs stretching down deep into the seabed, inspired the decks standing high above the sloping ground.

PLANS

I took my lead for this site from a garden we had created some years before, and set about planning a series of elevated decks in oval shapes set into the hill at different levels.

It was the concept of oil rigs that showed me how the deck supports should be anchored into the ground. I knew that digging foundations for the structures would be a nightmare in such a small space. The amount of excavation would be horrendous, and it's easy to do more harm than good by unsettling the soil and substructure. Pilings—used in the construction of oil rigs—were the answer. This is where steel pipes are sunk into the ground using enormous force, and filled with concrete. The rig platforms are then point-loaded on top of these pipes. Although expensive, this method would enable my platforms to be built quite easily. The decks themselves were to be made from lengths of reclaimed oak railroad ties edged in sleeves of stainless steel. I sketched them pointing in different directions to enhance the feeling of movement, and linked together by means of a wavy walkway and metal steps.

◄ ORIGINAL GARDEN
Because this steep, sloping garden was bordering on dangerous, I had to find a design solution that was dramatic but safe.

► SKETCHING IDEAS
First I sketched out fluid shapes—ellipses are often my starting point when I'm trying to create a sense of movement in a garden.

► SKETCHING IDEAS
The tiered, interlinking platforms are designed to lead the eye up to the top of the garden. The curved walkway adds to the dynamic effect.

◄ FINISHED GARDEN
The oval decks are rimmed with bands of stainless steel and, as an essential safety feature, enclosed by yacht handrails.

PLANTING LIST

CLOCKWISE FROM TOP LEFT

Euphorbia characias subsp. *wulfenii*

Beschorneria yuccoides

Stipa gigantea

Carex comans

Sasa veitchii

Taxus baccata 'Fastigiata'

Chamaerops humilis

The slopes surrounding the decks are planted with grasses, willows, and low-growing bamboos, including the beautiful cream-margined *Sasa veitchii*. I have also used drifts of *Euphorbia characias* subsp. *wulfenii*, which I love for its structural qualities and stately form.

I had an elliptical opening cut into the middle deck so that I could plant directly into the ground below. This adds interest to the deck and also means that the plants can tap into the moisture below the soil's surface and therefore need no additional watering once they are established. Through this aperture I planted a pencil-thin Italian cypress tree (*Cupressus sempervirens*), which has strong, vertical lines that create a striking contrast with the horizontal planes of the deck.

The sunny site is also ideal for succulents, such as agaves, which I used in large terracotta pots. Agaves are not hardy, but when planted in containers, they are easier to bring indoors over winter.

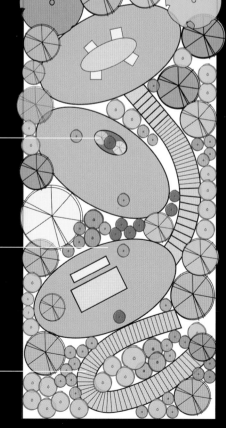

FINAL PLAN
Three oval oak decks provide practical areas to relax and play in this hillside garden

PLANTING HOLE
A cypress tree shoots through a hole in the deck

PLAYGROUND
Close to the house, the bottom deck is a play area for the children

SNAKING PATH
A winding path leads visitors into the garden

My clients had already tried to terrace this very steep site, so I went with the levels that they had partially created. Actually, these proved pretty useful because they provided a solid foundation on which to rest the back of each of the decks. This meant that I only had to support the front section to create the illusion of floating platforms.

I love water in gardens, but the original site was dangerously steep, and I felt that the addition of a waterfall, another potential hazard for children, was inappropriate. Instead, I have created the impression of water by using hundreds of tiny fiber-optic lights. These stream down the slope under the decks, and at night the effect is quite dazzling.

I often visit college graduation shows to pick up on new ideas and trends, and to spot talent; exhibitions and craft fairs are great places to find ideas, too. In this garden, I used tables and chairs by young designers, which I think really set off the design.

◄ DIFFICULT SITE

OPPOSITE PAGE MAIN PICTURE The sharp, steep slope in this small garden made terracing of some kind my only option. To dig out each terrace and remove the excess soil would have been a huge job, but the decks solve this problem because they are elevated on sturdy supports above the hilly land. I have used grasses and shrubs planted into the soil below the decks to soften the hard outlines of the structures and to create a multilayered effect.

◄ COMBINING OLD WITH NEW

OPPOSITE PAGE BELOW (THREE PICTURES) The oval decks combine traditional and modern materials. The natural wooden floors are edged with contrasting bands of stainless steel and yacht rails that catch the light and look particularly striking when set against a clear blue sky. I have introduced color into the design by painting the metal steps, which link the decks, a dark rusty red. The steps connect with wooden walkways that wind through the garden.

▲ DIFFERENT FUNCTIONS

ABOVE MAIN PICTURE Each of the garden's three decks has a different function, rather like rooms in a townhouse. The top deck, with the best view, is an outdoor dining room; the lower deck is a space for the children to use; and the one in the middle is for sunbathing and generally chilling out. I picked up the stylish spherical chairs on the central deck, which are made from terracotta, at a graduate show at the Royal College of Art in London.

▲ HIGH RISE

ABOVE (TWO PICTURES) Steep sites like this present a bit of a problem in terms of privacy—both yours and your neighbors'—so you have to think of the impact your design will have on everyone. I used palms and trees to help provide some sort of mutual screen. Planning permission is also an issue. In fact, you probably won't get it unless your design is not much higher than the existing slope or levels.

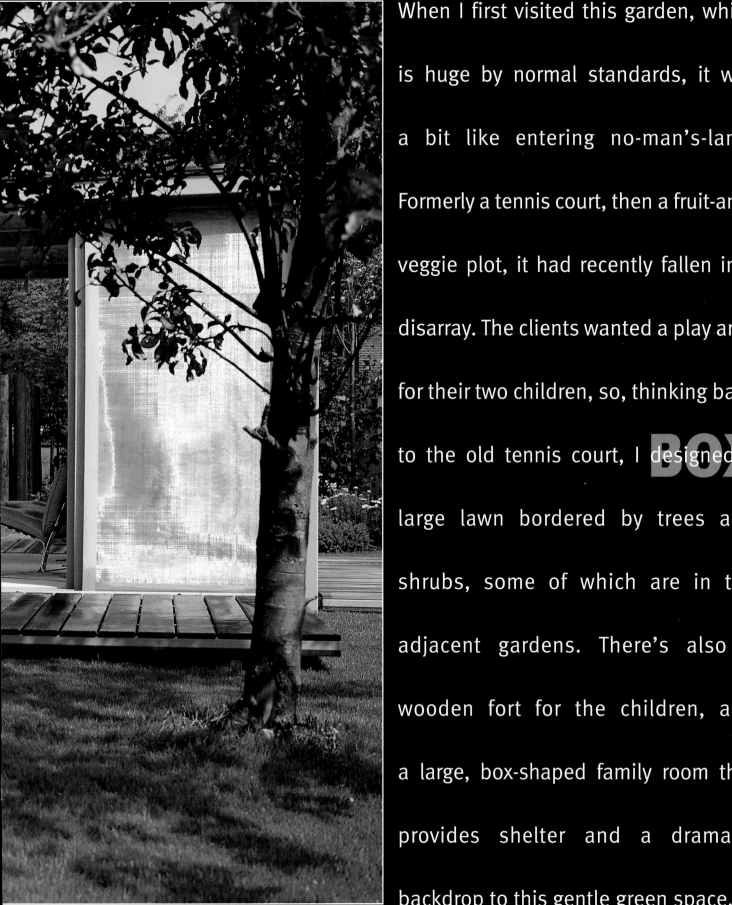

When I first visited this garden, which is huge by normal standards, it was a bit like entering no-man's-land. Formerly a tennis court, then a fruit-and-veggie plot, it had recently fallen into disarray. The clients wanted a play area for their two children, so, thinking back to the old tennis court, I designed a large lawn bordered by trees and shrubs, some of which are in the adjacent gardens. There's also a wooden fort for the children, and a large, box-shaped family room that provides shelter and a dramatic backdrop to this gentle green space.

BOX

The idea of a simple building appealed to me. Inspired by unlikely structures, such as horse boxes and shipping containers, I felt a large rectangular box would work well in this garden. There is something amusing about shipping containers: day and night they parade up and down the country, carried on trucks and trains, and then they are stacked like Lego blocks in ports before being shipped across the ocean on massive ships. It struck me that one of these utilitarian containers would make a perfect room—indeed, they're often used as sports changing rooms or temporary offices on building sites, and their value as cheap housing is also being explored. In the garden, I thought their blunt shape would contrast brilliantly with a soft lawn.

INSPIRATIONS

PLANS

There were hints about what should happen to this site. Planning permission existed for a tennis pavilion, and economics meant that it would make sense to reinstate the court by creating a top-notch lawn. The lawn could then be used as a children's play area and as host to a simple piece of architecture.

I wanted to delve into the idea of a pavilion, to understand its uses, to explore its potential as a garden room—a room that would be used occasionally and then locked up, coming to life when the family was in the garden. The building would be a wooden box that could be adapted for different uses, and would transform itself into an inviting, protected environment. It would also be an architectural backdrop for the garden.

Once the boundaries had been mapped out on paper, I drew the lines of a large rectangular lawn, and then, on top, I sketched in the boxlike structure. I also planned a second structure—a fort for the children to play in, its walls formed from a palisade of telephone poles. More poles could be used at the other end of the garden, but this time as seats, lying on the ground.

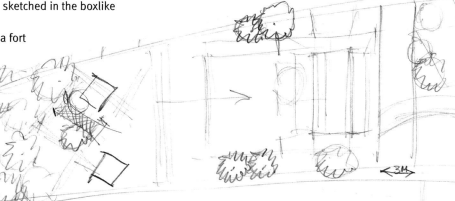

▲ SKETCHING IDEAS
There was already planning permission for a tennis pavilion, which inspired the idea of a long, low building. The fold-down walls would allow it to be opened up on warm, sunny days.

▼ SKETCHING IDEAS
I mapped out the boundaries, figured out where the large, rectangular lawn would go, and then played around with possible sites for the pavilion.

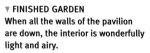

▼ FINISHED GARDEN
When all the walls of the pavilion are down, the interior is wonderfully light and airy.

▼ SKETCHING IDEAS
I decided to use the building as a central focal point, its wooden walls standing out against a green carpet of grass.

To create privacy in the garden, I planned a mass planting of small trees, such as hornbeam (*Carpinus*), birch (*Betula*), and rowan (*Sorbus*). These are concentrated in the more exposed areas, behind the fort and along the borders that run parallel to the boundaries. Shrubs provide a lower story of greenery. Tough evergreens, such as *Aucuba japonica* 'Crotonifolia', with its splotched and splashed leaves, add a dash of color all through winter. In summer, clematis, passion flowers (*Passiflora*), and other climbers, such as the Chilean potato vine (*Solanum crispum* 'Glasnevin'), twine and tangle among the branches to make an even denser curtain of camouflage.

PLANTS

PLANTING LIST

CLOCKWISE FROM TOP LEFT
Solanum crispum 'Glasnevin'
Hypericum 'Hidcote'
Passiflora 'Amethyst'
Hosta fortunei var. *aureomarginata*
Clematis 'Arabella'
Potentilla fruticosa 'Goldfinger'
Aucuba japonica 'Crotonifolia'

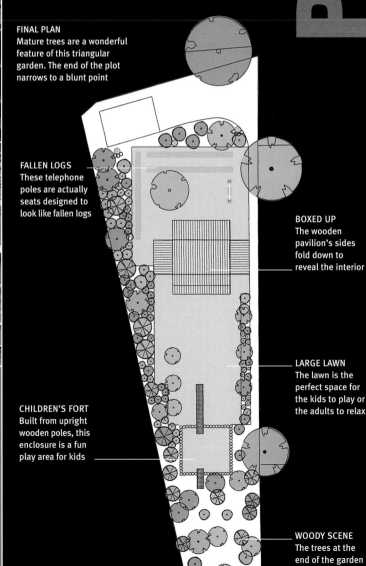

FINAL PLAN
Mature trees are a wonderful feature of this triangular garden. The end of the plot narrows to a blunt point

FALLEN LOGS
These telephone poles are actually seats designed to look like fallen logs

BOXED UP
The wooden pavilion's sides fold down to reveal the interior

LARGE LAWN
The lawn is the perfect space for the kids to play or the adults to relax

CHILDREN'S FORT
Built from upright wooden poles, this enclosure is a fun play area for kids

WOODY SCENE
The trees at the end of the garden are clearly visible behind the fort

Although this garden was, in one sense, always going to be a semi-public space—because the clients wanted it to be a play area for both their children and their children's friends—the fact that 20 households directly overlook the plot dictated the need for some privacy.

To achieve this, the wooden box can be opened or shut on all sides, so that the family can choose when they want to be screened from the neighbors. The walls are attached to the box at the bottom with heavy, sprung hinges—like the ones used on horse boxes. These allow one person to pull down the panels and lay them safely on the ground to form a temporary deck. When all the panels are down, a second, inner skin made of wood and stainless-steel mesh provides weather and bug protection. The building, therefore, is flexible and can meet different needs by adopting different configurations. In the evening, after a good day's play, tennis rackets, footballs, and furniture can be packed into the box and all the sides closed up.

At the other end of the garden, an architectural steel-grille tunnel leads into the fort, which is constructed from telephone poles sunk into the ground. The fort is a semi-private area for the children, and its square shape mirrors the box, helping to unify the overall design.

▲ POLE FORT

ABOVE The fort is at the bottom of the garden and the children love to play in this space, shielded both from their parents and the neighbors. The tunnel through which they enter the fort is made from galvanized steel mesh, and provides a wonderful textural contrast with the wooden poles.

Colorful disks break up the swath of lawn. They're not fixed to the ground, and the children use them to play a game they invented based on hopscotch.

▼ METAMORPHOSES

BELOW (SIX PICTURES) The box room has infinite uses. On cool days, one wall panel can be lowered to allow light and air in while the remaining panels keep the box warm and dry. On sunny days, with all panels down and the screens pulled back, the box is surrounded by decked terraces. It is a perfect place for a party: the screens deter bugs yet allow the garden scents to filter through. And when the guests are gone, it offers a cool, relaxing retreat.

◄ IN THE FRAME

TOP LEFT AND LEFT This garden is designed as a practical space in which to relax and play, but I also love its graphic quality. Simplicity is the key to the design: angular hard landscaping, pleasing proportions, and unfussy lines all have a calming effect. The geometric architecture also frames different views, and the box is like the backdrop of a stage set, intensifying the performance of the trees, log seats, and lawn.

▲ REPEATED THEMES

ABOVE Horizontal telephone poles—in keeping with the geometric lines of the garden—are used as seats.

I planted small trees, such as rowans and birches, between the poles and the structures. These complement mature trees in neighboring gardens and create an overall sylvan theme. In time, these new trees will provide additional privacy, while contributing to the color in the garden with foliage, blossom, and berries.

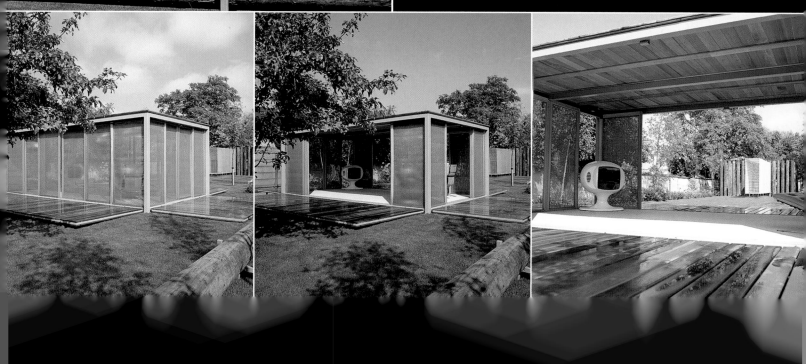

These gardens are where the imagination is
set free and the craziest of ideas become reality. DREAM
Close your eyes and journey into dreamland

Inspired by a dream about shark fins, I had long harbored the idea of huge, rusting metal structures rising up from a lawn. Then I met Kaya, a photographer, who wanted a private space in her garden where she wouldn't be overlooked. The huge steel fin—dangerous, sharp, and emerging ominously from a pool of still water—was my solution. Dramatic and exciting, it also acts as a screen behind which I hid a secret space. Here, masked by metal and lush foliage, I installed a spa, with hot tub and shower, for the ultimate luxury retreat.

SHARK'S FIN

INSPIRATIONS

Kaya, my client, knew that she wanted a garden with lush planting and a tropical feel, to remind her of vacations, but beyond that she couldn't really give me a brief because she had no reference points. She presented me with the perfect opportunity to use a shape I had dreamt about years before, and which had followed me around ever since—the shark's fin. A finlike sculpture that would scare people a bit, too, soon became the dominant theme for my design.

Kaya lived on a suburban street, overlooked by rows of houses, so the need for privacy, a space that wasn't overlooked, was paramount. She also wanted an area to relax, and I was inspired by outdoor hot tubs and showers that I'd seen in magazines. I decided to use these, shielded by the giant fin sculpture.

PLANS

Site location is an important factor in every project, but it had special significance for Kaya. Surrounded by rows of suburban houses, her garden was totally overlooked by other people's windows, and she wanted some privacy—easy to achieve indoors where you can pull the curtains, but much harder outside.

Lush planting was one way of tackling the problem, but the giant shark's fin that I wanted to incorporate was a more interesting, less obvious solution. Made of steel, the fin was to have a dual purpose: to act as a doorway, and as a divider to a secret space complete with hot tub and shower. I designed a surfboard-shaped bridge to cross the pond in front of the fin. This would be portable—with a handle cut into it—and act like a key, allowing Kaya exclusive access to her own secret garden.

I wanted water somewhere else in the garden and decided to update the idea of an Islamic-style rill for my contemporary design. Girders, curved by a foundry I knew of in Birmingham, offered me a way of creating a modern, delicately rippling water feature.

▲ ORIGINAL GARDEN
My brief was to introduce more structure and a private area into this long, rectangular plot.

► SKETCHING IDEAS
I'd been waiting for the right opportunity to use the shark's fin in a garden design—that time came when my client told me she wanted a secluded area. I just had to fit it into my other ideas for the site.

▼ MODEL GARDEN
I used the shark's fin to screen off an area at the back of the garden. A bridge in the shape of a surfboard leads to a doorway in the fin.

▼ FINISHED GARDEN
A leaf-shaped lawn, edged by lush beds, directs you into the garden.

When you're faced with a garden with very few features, the idea is to create interest with planting. The elevated, leaf-shaped lawns seesaw from right to left across this garden, drawing people in, and the shark's fin toward the back is bulked out with planting. I have also made the garden look bigger by using groups of plants to disguise the boundaries, and to direct people's eyes into, and through, the garden.

I have used a joyous mixture of plants with lots of color, form, and structure—as a photographer, Kaya has a great eye for this. One border is mainly tropical, and features Australian grasses and the tree fern *Dicksonia antarctica*; the other border is mixed and packed with perovskias, hostas, astilbes, and a beautiful *Trachycarpus fortunei*.

A really committed plantswoman, Kaya looks after her garden carefully. I planted a mature eucalyptus—a tree that is notoriously difficult to transplant successfully—and even this is doing really well.

PLANTING LIST

CLOCKWISE FROM TOP LEFT
Ligularia przewalskii
Perovskia 'Blue Spire'
Jubaea chilensis
Trachycarpus fortunei
Zantedeschia elliottiana
Dryopteris
Astilbe x *arendsii* 'Fanal'

FINAL PLAN
Two lawns arc across the garden, dividing up the space and defining use

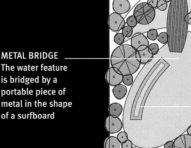

HOT WATER
An octagonal hot tub is hidden from neighbors by the shark's fin

METAL BRIDGE
The water feature is bridged by a portable piece of metal in the shape of a surfboard

CURVED RILLS
Two curved, shallow rills, painted red, add a touch of drama

RAISED LAWN
The raised lawn is in the shape of a leaf and leads into the garden

FIRST STEPS
A wooden deck is used for entertaining

The shark's fin garden defined my style for a few years. The fin followed me around to many design meetings, making its presence felt long after I had left it behind. It seems to galvanize opinion, both for and against a particular style of design that I like to work with, and for a while I thought I would never escape it.

This garden is often misunderstood by people who have not visited it. Now, I'm not saying that everyone would like this garden if they wandered through it—indeed, I think that feeling would be reserved for a distinct minority—but the importance of understanding the site, the situation and the client's needs are clear in this space.

Kaya, my client, was delighted with the finished design and enjoyed the garden to the full. It is modern, but the soft lawns and planting temper the madness of the fin and the surfboard bridge, and it is an easy garden to live with.

▲ BLUE HUES

ABOVE (TWO PICTURES) I decided to paint the house wall a deep marine blue— it's a rich color that works brilliantly as a backdrop to the lush planting and smooth, green, tiered lawns. The strong blue also reflects onto the plants themselves, giving them an almost surreal pigmentation. The blue in the perovskia, for example, is intensified and creates a startling contrast against the striking yellow-leaved choisya.

◄ INTIMATE ENCLOSURE

LEFT (THREE PICTURES) Hidden behind the shark's fin is a secluded sanctuary where the client is screened from the neighbors. The hot shower installed here provides the perfect way to unwind after a day at work—an invigorating atmosphere is created by the blend of water and scents from ferns and other planting.

The shark imagery spills over onto the lawns, with their rills made from girders. These are set into the grass and painted a deep blood red.

► SAFE SURFING

OPPOSITE PAGE (FIVE PICTURES) Toying with the rather sinister concept behind the garden design, I thought another macabre touch would be to run a surfboard-shaped bridge across the pool to the opening in the shark's fin.

To heighten the drama, I have used striking flowers and foliage— such as the tall yellow spikes of ligularias, glaucous-leaved hostas, and straplike phormiums. Reflected in the pool in front of the fin, their presence is effectively duplicated.

The aperture in the shark's fin doubles as a doorway and framing device that defines a vivid snapshot of the garden.

A wooden deck, running across the back of the house, offers an ideal vantage point from which to view the garden. The rigid wood surface strongly contrasts with the soft, fluid lawn and planting. It also provides a space for dining and can easily accommodate a table and four chairs.

DETAILS

On my first visit to this garden, I was struck by the clear, open skies, criss-crossed with trails from airplanes on their way to and from the nearby airport. The plot itself looked like a lumberyard, but despite the debris, it had a serenity that suggested it had once been beautiful. The clients wanted a contemporary outdoor space, but rather than remove the character of the garden, I enhanced it using existing features—such as the 100-year-old horse chestnut tree—together with modern steel and glass forms inspired by the planes flying above.

AIRPLANE

INSPIRATIONS

Modern transportation methods were the thrust behind my design. The main influence was the airplanes that flew low over the area; but the client, who ran a helicopter shuttle service for Formula One race meetings, also inspired ideas.

On my regular commute between London and Dublin, I often gaze out at the sleek wings of the plane, marveling at how they manage to keep such a massive piece of machinery airborne. No garden I build is ever going to take off, but I felt that by using the plane's smooth, slim shape in my design, I would achieve the appearance of dynamism.

Bus shelters were another key concept. I love their contemporary design and felt their glass walls could be translated into a wonderful garden structure.

A modern, glass-sided conservatory ran along the back of the house, jutting out into the garden space. Standing inside, looking out at the planes flying overhead, I felt as though I was on the observation deck of an airport. I found this exhilarating, and was inspired to design raised flower beds around the boundaries, complete with retaining walls topped with satin-polished, stainless-steel bumpers, shaped like the leading edge of an aircraft wing.

Steel can look cold and severe on damp, gray days, so to counter this, I decided to use warm-colored pavers for the patio bordering the house, and plenty of plants, including ornamental grasses and tree ferns, to soften the overall effect. At night, neon strip lights would bathe the garden in a warm glow.

The main focal point of the design was to be a glass-sided room, which I based on a bus shelter and positioned in the middle of a lawn. Safely cocooned from the British weather, I imagined the clients relaxing inside it, enjoying the plants or reading a book. In front, I designed a rectangular bed surrounded by a rill.

▶ **SKETCHING IDEAS**
The planes that fly overhead were the inspiration for the winglike roof on top of the main garden structure.

▼ **FINISHED DESIGN**
The completed garden has a very sleek, aerodynamic quality to it, while the plants add a tropical feel.

▲ **MODEL GARDEN**
I decided to build the garden room's walls in glass, supported by metal poles. I wanted airport-like lighting to play its part, too.

The planting on this project was hugely influenced by my client. An avid gardener, she had lived in a flat for a year while waiting for this house to be remodeled and was desperate to get back into the garden. Despite living without any outdoor space for such a long time, she had still managed to collect loads of cuttings and plants in pots, which she brought to her new home. We needed more, however, so I took her shopping to choose a few new ones. She liked both old-fashioned and new-style plants, and this is reflected in her choice of heucheras, dicksonias, and phormiums.

We had to work around a huge chestnut tree that stands in the garden, and bought plants that thrive in the shade, including ferns and hostas. In the partial shade nearby, the particularly pretty Japanese mock orange (*Pittosporum tobira*) flowers in late spring and early summer. And in a sunny spot I've used a beautiful callicarpa.

PLANTS

PLANTING LIST

CLOCKWISE FROM TOP LEFT
Dicksonia antarctica
Callicarpa bodinieri var. *giraldii*
 'Profusion'
Phormium 'Sundowner'
Phormium cookianum
 'Variegatum'
Liquidambar styraciflua

FINAL PLAN
The garden's boundaries formed a flared L-shape, which made it an interesting design proposition

WATER FEATURE
A shallow water-filled rill runs around the perimeter of this planting trough

GARDEN ROOM
The glass room sits in the middle of the lawn, offering 360° views of the garden

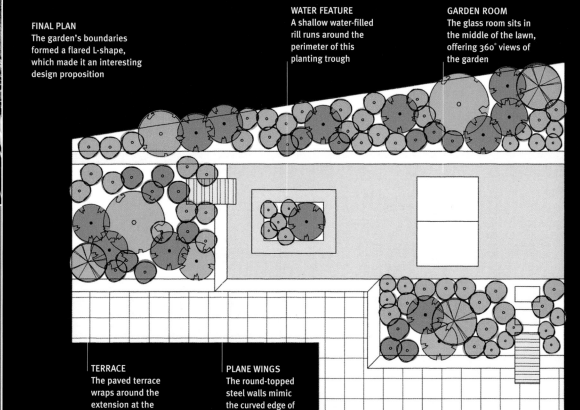

TERRACE
The paved terrace wraps around the extension at the back of the house

PLANE WINGS
The round-topped steel walls mimic the curved edge of an airplane wing

The restored period house has a sleek, modern, brick and glass extension, and the completely separate garden room is made of state-of-the-art materials. The idea is that if you're in the extension you can admire the garden with its garden room, and if you're in the garden room you can admire the extension and the house. I love the mix of old and new in all the spaces, and it is interesting to see how well the manufactured stainless-steel retaining walls work with the natural Portland stone I used for the patios.

Changes in light—whether natural or artificial—have an enormous effect on the garden and its architecture. Lights sunk into the lawn, underneath the roll of the stainless-steel topped walls, and in the pool under the grille floor of the garden room, look amazing as they reflect upward. I wanted to install a small pump in the garden-room pool so that it would create ripples and the lights would project a wavy image onto the metal ceiling above.

DETAILS

▲ REFLECTIONS OF THE SKY

ABOVE An island bed takes on new meaning here. The square water feature is constructed from anodized aluminum and contains about 3in (8cm) of water—just enough to reflect the sky. Architectural planting is set into the middle of the bed.

Lighting is sunk into the lawn underneath the protruding, curved steel walls—the reflections at night are quite startling.

Metal steps, like those used to board planes, allow easy access between the different terraced levels.

◄ LIGHTING UP

OPPOSITE PAGE Neon strip lighting illuminates the garden in hot magenta and cool blue—the metal and glass surfaces bounce the colors and light around the garden.

Inside the glass shelter, a metal grille floor is set over a pool of water which, again, is lit up at night.

► ROLLED METAL

RIGHT (FOUR PICTURES) Influenced by the airplanes that fly overhead on their way to and from the nearby airport, I capped the retaining walls with stainless steel shaped into a winglike form. These jet wings have an immediate and dramatic visual impact—take a closer look and you'll see that they also capture the busy skyscape in their reflective surfaces.

A small, rectangular lawn defines one of the terraced levels, while the patio follows the angles of the modern glass and metal extension. Both areas are well-defined, with crisp, neat edges.

To complement the contemporary tastes of my clients and the modern, sometimes even clubby, feel of the rest of the garden, I installed a bench by furniture designer Simon Percival. Not only does it offer a comfortable place to sit and enjoy the surrounding space, but its sleek shape perfectly echoes the overall design.

The family was normal; their home wasn't. On my first visit, I was amazed by their grand Art Deco concrete house, with its flat roof and solarium, although an ugly extension at the back marred its beauty. The garden was bland, with a lawn, shed, and not much else. My initial idea was a garden in the style of Luis Barragán or Frank Lloyd Wright, but instead, a flamboyant design evolved: an over-the-top celebration of decadence and fun, with a pink and red terrazzo patio, tiered lawns, blue-tiled pools, and a lemon-shaped, glitterball cocktail cabinet.

HOLLYWOOD

INSPIRATIONS

Sometimes a total fantasy jumps up and hits you in the face. Here, it was the glitz and glamour of Hollywood movies of the 1930s and 1940s. My ideas were gleaned from the stylish Busby Berkeley film sets of that time, starlets draped in ostrich feathers, Art Deco designs, and the swanky American Bar at London's Savoy Hotel. Those glamorous, ornamental pools at the Hotel Bel-Air in Los Angeles helped to define the style, too.

I also needed a focal point—a statue or piece of sculpture. Then I remembered a U2 concert, when the group emerged from a giant lemon-shaped glitterball. This inspired the idea of a mirrored cocktail cabinet—more 1920s than rock 'n' roll. And, like Joe 90's electron device, it would revolve and reflect light.

PLANS

I expected to go down the road of creating lots of white plastered walls in the austere 1930s style, but there was something about the clients and their young children that just spelled fun. As much as I tried to draw stark pavilions and perfectly rectangular lawns that would match the house, other ideas—most notably the fan or shell shape—just wouldn't go away, and in the end I couldn't fight them. As a result, my plans became much more over-the-top than I had expected, and the whole thing just came together as I started to sketch these shapes. A natural symmetry wanted to assert itself and this, at least, had a 1930s feel—in fact, my idea to use terrazzo for the patio was to explore a luxurious material that was being used widely during that era.

When I went back to the clients and told them what I wanted to do, they were pretty surprised—they even laughed—but they went with it. I then had to just squeeze in a play area for the children at the back of the plot.

◄ ORIGINAL GARDEN
My clients wanted me to transform their ordinary back garden into something stylish and glamorous.

◄ SKETCHING IDEAS
Ideas for this garden hit me immediately, taking shape in my sketchbook in a matter of moments. I looked for ways to reinterpret the glitz of 1930s and 1940s Hollywood.

▲ MODEL GARDEN
From the way the tiered, shell-like curves of the lawn fan out from the patio, it's easy to see that the geometric forms of Art Deco were an influence on my design.

▶ FINISHED DESIGN
Flanked by sparkling blue water, the garden's glittering focal point is the silver-colored cocktail cabinet, which stands like a giant lemon at the end of the main section of lawn.

This is a fun design, and the planting reflects that. The first and most obvious element is the theatrical series of stepped lawns. Such large areas of grass on so many different levels can be awkward to mow, but practice makes perfect. Boxwood (*Buxus sempervirens*) is planted *en masse* behind the pool. The idea is that it will eventually be clipped, Japanese style, into cloud shapes to add to the cinematic feel of the garden—clipping box into basic, free-form shapes like these is a skill that becomes easier each time you do it.

To counter these two slightly tricky maintenance issues, I deliberately tried to cut down on the work needed in the rest of the garden. There are spiky phormiums in some of the borders, and the two beds on either side of the terrazzo patio are filled with glamorous, pink seasonal flowers: hyacinths in spring; petunias during the summer; and primulas or pansies during the winter.

PLANTING LIST

CLOCKWISE FROM TOP LEFT

Buxus sempervirens
Skimmia japonica
Fatsia japonica
Viburnum davidii
Ilex aquifolium 'Golden Queen'

FINAL PLAN
A large area of this garden comprises a shell-shaped lawn surrounded by water

REFRESHMENTS
The huge, lemon-shaped sculpture opens to reveal a liquor cabinet

WATER FEATURE
A blue-tiled pool looks glamorous even on a dull winter's day

PLAY APPARATUS
In the corner of the garden, a climbing frame is masked by plants

GREEN SCENE
Evergreen plants help to define the tiled water feature

TIERED LAWNS
The tiered lawns echo '30s and '40s Hollywood film sets

TERRAZZO PATIO
This curved pink and red terrazzo patio is inlaid with lines of brass

I originally wanted a statue, rather than a cocktail cabinet, to be the centerpiece of the garden. I imagined a beautiful design, maybe a figurative lady with elegant sweeping lines rising from the ground at the flick of a switch. But time, money, and other events conspired against me, while health and safety issues were also proving difficult, with the fear of children getting stuck in the trapdoors. In the end, this Hollywood vision morphed into a giant glitterball—a revolving sphere positioned toward the end of the main lawn.

Although the cocktail cabinet is a bit of a compromise, the curved patio in pink and red terrazzo with inlaid lines of brass is exactly right. Extremely glamorous, terrazzo is made up of polished chips of marble set into a shiny compound, and is best known as the material into which the stars on Hollywood Boulevard Walk of Fame are inlaid. Here, it provides the perfect surface for a vibrant, over-the-top patio.

◄ SIMPLE DESIGN

OPPOSITE PAGE FAR LEFT Simple designs often create the best effects. Here, even in the winter months, the structural elements of this garden work their visual magic. The shiny silver panels of the garden's lemon-shaped liquor cabinet, for example, reflect the changing colors of the sky and the surrounding plants. When splashed with rain, the drops on the mirrors take on a jewel-like quality.

◄ TIERED CURVES

OPPOSITE PAGE LEFT Late in the year, British skies may be gray and dreary but the turquoise and cobalt-blue tiles used to line the pools reflect color and light, infusing the garden with glamour whatever the weather. I also love the juxtaposition of these cool pools against the curved, tiered, emerald lawns, which together give the design a distinct rhythmic pattern.

As well as looking really stylish, the uncluttered areas of grass also contribute to a sense of openness.

OPEN AIR ▲

ABOVE AND RIGHT (THREE PICTURES) This is primarily a garden for adults to enjoy, but I also wanted to introduce a sense of humor and fun. The clients were amazed and amused by the lemon-shaped cocktail cabinet, which opens to reveal a full stock of liquor and mixers. They wanted to party in the garden, and this cabinet certainly sets the scene for a soirée. When the children have their friends over, the cabinet can be filled with soft drinks and candy.

Also for the children, I have included a wooden climbing frame, half hidden behind the shrubs, so it doesn't detract from the main design.

The fountains finish off the glamorous theme, and add to the sensory experience of the garden. Moving water is one of the most important elements of urban garden design, and the sound of these fountains helps to screen out traffic and other noise pollutants. They also light up like fireworks at night.

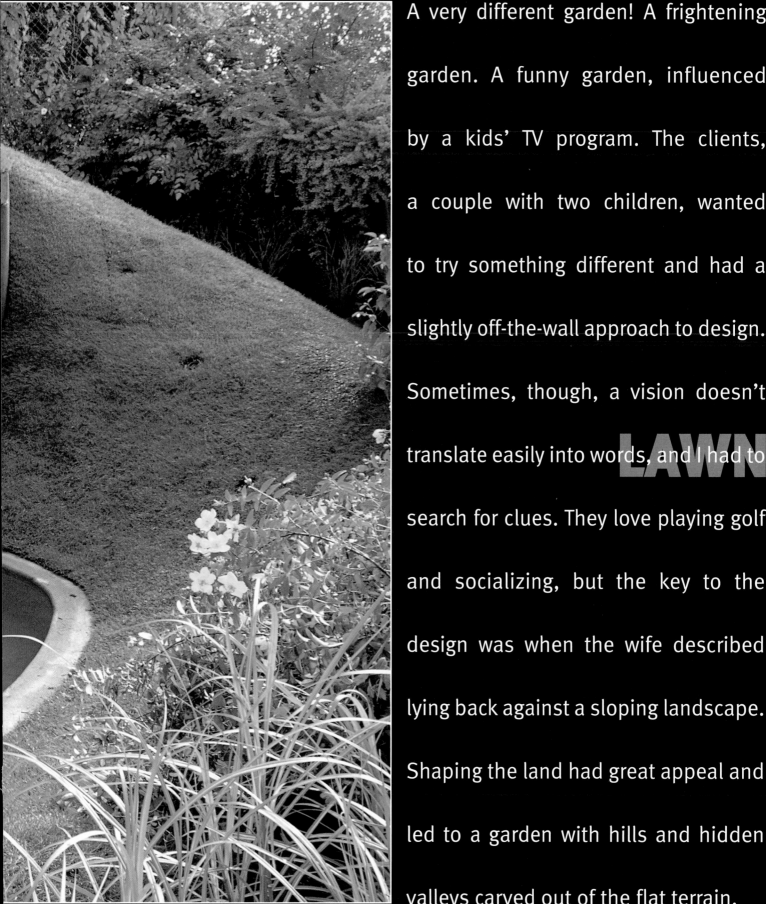

A very different garden! A frightening garden. A funny garden, influenced by a kids' TV program. The clients, a couple with two children, wanted to try something different and had a slightly off-the-wall approach to design. Sometimes, though, a vision doesn't translate easily into words, and I had to search for clues. They love playing golf and socializing, but the key to the design was when the wife described lying back against a sloping landscape. Shaping the land had great appeal and led to a garden with hills and hidden valleys carved out of the flat terrain.

LAWN

INSPIRATIONS

The idea of lying back against a hill captured my imagination, and my thoughts turned to shaping the land and changing its form. I had also long been frustrated with suburban gardens—usually rectangular and laid out conventionally—which exist in yard after yard, street after street, town after town. But watching American and Australian soap operas, I noticed something different: the gardens shown in them have no real boundaries, just carved land, with lawn running up to a slope at the end of a plot, delineating a boundary.

Golf courses also came to mind—those manufactured landscapes molded into Lilliputian kingdoms of hills, hollows, and plains. Sunglasses, the curves of a paisley pattern, Capability Brown landscapes— but more surreal, never trying to be natural—and the designs of Charles Jencks also merged to create this extreme garden.

THE GARDEN OF COSMIC SPECULATION
CHARLES JENCKS

I took a pad and sketched, and sketched, and sketched until I came up with an idea I believed would work for this free-form garden. Carving and shaping the land in three dimensions, I tried to create elegant, sculptural shapes for people to travel through.

I wanted a mini-landscape filled with mountains and a cave made from, and hidden by, molded soil. The cave would create a usable, half-concealed den at the sunny end of the garden, perfect for entertaining, which was an important part of the clients' lifestyle. To make the den more comfortable, I planned for a stereo, and to ensure it could be used year-round, I decided to install a stove with a chimney that emerged from the lawn above.

Outside the back door I designed a patio laid on a diagonal grid that would increase the sense of space and provide a flat surface to contrast with the steep gradients of the mounds.

▲ ORIGINAL GARDEN
The garden was a typical rectangular suburban yard with a central lawn flanked by narrow borders and trees.

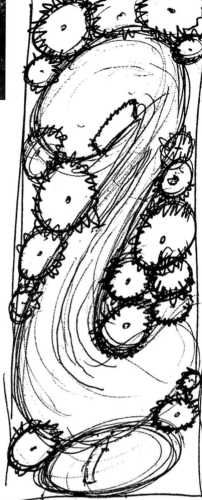

► SKETCHING IDEAS
Sensuous curves dominated my initial thoughts, and gradually the shape of an enormous back-to-front 'S' emerged in my sketches.

◄ MODEL GARDEN
Building models is especially useful for projects where the ground isn't flat. This may mean working with a steep slope, but here it meant creating a series of contours.

◄ FINISHED DESIGN
The mound curves just as the model shows, but in reality it is smooth and covered in sod.

This garden is not just about the way the plants look; it's also about the sounds they make. I have filled areas around the mounds with ornamental grasses that sway in the breeze and make soothing, rustling sounds, which echo the swishing of the birch canopies.

Color, form, and texture are important, too, and the grasses I've put together include all three elements. Broad, stiff types rub shoulders with tall, narrow species with feathery seed heads. I chose varieties for their colors as well; these range from greens and reds to buffs and brilliant orange.

The clients aren't avid gardeners and the planting reflects this: ornamental grasses don't need much care. The main maintenance is mowing the grass on the mounds, and although this is a little tricky, the clients have now gotten it down to a fine art.

PLANTING LIST

CLOCKWISE FROM TOP LEFT

Helictotrichon sempervirens
Stipa tenuissima
Stipa arundinacea
Miscanthus sinensis 'Malepartus'
Prunus lusitanica
Betula
Phalaris arundinacea var. *picta* 'Feesey'

FINAL PLAN
Two mounds linked by a ridge evoke gentle rolling hills

HIDEY-HOLE
A cavelike hut is carved out of the earth and hidden beneath the lawn

REFLECTING POOL
An oval pool sits neatly at the foot of the hill at the end of the yard

RUSTLING GRASS
Many different grasses rustle in the wind at the base of the hills

GREEN CARPET
The mounds are carpeted with a lush green lawn

CREATING SPACE
Paving slabs laid on the diagonal increase the

The finished garden is probably beyond description—you have to be there to really understand it. The most important thing for me is that, whatever anyone else may think, I have met the clients' brief: shaping the land outside their door into something special, and creating a social center in a garden that's hard to get to, which is an achievement to reach. Negotiating your way around the garden, causing people to stop in their tracks when they see what's there, challenging expectations, making people smile, maybe even getting people angry—this is the result. But the bottom line is that the clients have a new garden, built just for them, that they really love.

Is it practical? Perhaps not. It's not easy to get around, but should every place be easy? Mowing the grass is a fine art and takes just under an hour. The design is certainly adventurous, definitely fun, but it did require a huge amount of bravery from the clients.

◄ CREATING VISTAS

OPPOSITE PAGE (SIX PICTURES) This garden is a contained and undulating landscape in miniature, with two main mounds softly contoured and joined in the middle by a ridge. Together they create a three-dimensional S-shape that snakes along the length of the garden, reaching almost from one end to the other. Only visible once you have climbed the first hill, a cavelike shelter hidden beneath the farthest hump is

The view from the top of this second hill offers a new perspective of the garden. At night, it is illuminated by lights sunk into the ridge—recessed to let a lawn mower glide over them— that highlight the garden's features.

The cave, with its wood-burning stove, offers warmth and shelter in winter and shade from the midday sun in summer, while the paved area close to the house provides another outdoor

▲ HIDDEN SANCTUARY

THIS PAGE (THREE PICTURES) The sensuous curves of the landscaping contrast with the regimented paving slabs outside the house. Laid on the diagonal to create a sense of greater width and to draw people into the garden, the slabs are divided by strips of sod and dotted with young silver birches and the occasional shrub.

I planted hundreds of ornamental grasses around the edge of the garden

birches. As they quiver and rustle in the breeze, they bring sound and movement into the garden.

Visually, the hills create harmony, but in practical terms they also provide the perfect place to lie back and enjoy the sun. And they also make an exciting landscape for children to explore.

The oval doorway to the cave mirrors the shape of the pool and, when sitting inside the den, becomes a perfect

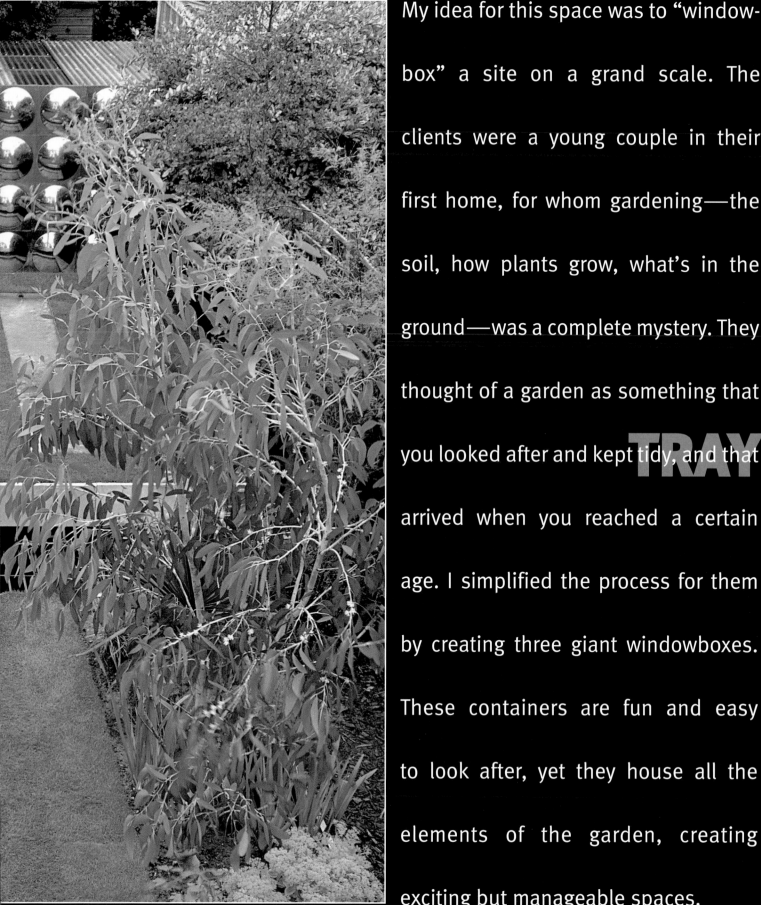

My idea for this space was to "window-box" a site on a grand scale. The clients were a young couple in their first home, for whom gardening—the soil, how plants grow, what's in the ground—was a complete mystery. They thought of a garden as something that you looked after and kept tidy, and that arrived when you reached a certain age. I simplified the process for them by creating three giant windowboxes. These containers are fun and easy to look after, yet they house all the elements of the garden, creating exciting but manageable spaces.

TRAY

My first idea for this garden was to create gigantic window boxes, but another key influence for the trays was the world's most famous private house—Frank Lloyd Wright's "Fallingwater" in Pennsylvania. The house, set above a waterfall and surrounded by beautiful woodland, has huge balconies that float out from the main structure and look as if they're defying gravity. I had also seen customized cars with neon lights installed below the chassis, and used this same lighting effect under the trays.

The garden was in need of a backdrop to set it off. I wanted to cover the wooden workshop at the back of the plot with stainless-steel panels in a bubble pattern I'd seen on a building on a traffic roundabout in London. The idea crystallized when I saw photos of rock musician Lenny Kravitz's house in Miami, which is clad in similar bubble paneling.

INSPIRATIONS

PLANS

Plants can thrive in surprisingly shallow soil, so my plan for this garden was to create giant trays that would contain all the soft landscaping. These trays needed to be made from strong and durable materials, because the combined weight of the soil and plants would be phenomenal. I planned to use hardwood, bound with steel, and raise them off the ground on legs made from girders set into deep concrete.

To create the ideal conditions for as wide a range of plants as possible, the trays would be filled with a mixture of garden soil and compost. And at 18in (45cm) deep, the trays could accommodate most things—grass, for example, will grow well in just 8in (20cm) of good-quality topsoil, while shrubs and herbaceous perennials need a depth of up to 12in (30cm). But I wanted more height, and that meant big plants. To accommodate them, I designed a large aperture in one of the raised trays, so you could peer down to ground level, with three birch trees shooting out of it. I thought the trees' white trunks would look great framed by the steel-rimmed opening, and their foliage, which would normally be well above head height, could be viewed up close. I designed a second tray to house a mixed border.

▲ ORIGINAL GARDEN
This garden was a blank canvas with a no-frills lawn and minimal planting. The water-filled tub was the only feature.

▼ SKETCHING IDEAS
Outlining the trays was like a study in perspective drawing. They help elongate the view, drawing the eye to the metal screen which, with its circular motif, is a strong visual end to the garden.

▼ FINISHED DESIGN
The interlocking trays create height in an otherwise flat site, offering new perspectives and planting opportunities.

▲ MODEL GARDEN
When I saw my design in 3-D, it was interesting to see how the trays slotted together like a series of giant stepping stones.

The trays in this garden illustrate the fact that you don't need huge depths of soil to grow plants. Just look at roof gardens, like the one on top of the former "Derry and Toms" department store on Kensington High Street, London, where mature trees, including a chestnut, grow in relatively shallow soil, probably less than 2½ft (75cm).

Full borders of mixed planting flank the lawn in the first lower tray, their growth sustained by good irrigation and feeding. The borders feature a range of beautiful plants, including the red-hot poker, *Kniphofia caulescens*, pink achilleas, lavenders, and a blue-leaved multistemmed *Eucalyptus gunnii*. In small suburban gardens, it's good to have interest throughout the year, and eucalyptus is perfect for this because it keeps its foliage over winter. The upper tray is dominated by three white-stemmed birches that burst through a hole from the soil below.

PLANTING LIST

CLOCKWISE FROM TOP LEFT
Sedum Autumn Joy
Eucalyptus gunnii
Phyllostachys nigra
Achillea millefolium 'Cerise Queen'
Cotinus coggygria 'Royal Purple'
Kniphofia caulescens
Lavandula angustifolia 'Hidcote'

FINAL PLAN
A beautiful garden, complete with a stream and grassy glades, is contained within the three giant trays

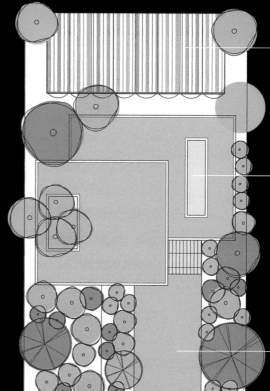

WORKSHOP
Polished metal cladding turns a mundane building into a work of art

MOVING WATER
A shallow steel-lined rill captures the reflection of the sky overhead

MINI-LAWNS
Each tray was sodded to create three smooth, level lawns

A recurring theme in many of my designs is the illusion of defying gravity, and that's definitely a big part of this garden. The idea is that the three platforms or trays appear to hover above the ground at different heights. The trays house all the elements of a traditional garden—including soil, lawns, trees, borders, even a small stream—and designing them was similar to making a roof garden, where weight distribution is an extremely important issue and careful consideration must be given to drainage.

The shed clad with stainless-steel tiles provides a funky backdrop. To create this wonderful bubble effect, a sheet of steel is turned on a wheel at high speed and a piece of wood is dragged across it.

Other features in the garden include a sculptural molded concrete bench. Made to a secret lightweight recipe, I chose it because its fluid lines contrast so well with the angular trays.

It took a lot of work to build this garden—constructing the elevated trays was a feat of engineering—but it was worth it, and I like its clean, sharp edges. To me it is a sculptural space, where all the elements work together to create a garden of elegant proportions.

DETAILS

◄ GEOMETRIC TRAYS

OPPOSITE PAGE (FIVE PICTURES) Constructed from steel and wood, the trays are defined by the cool brushed metal edges which, at night, are illuminated from below with blue neon lights. The hard edges are also designed to contrast with the soft texture of the lawns. Three silver birches offer an element of surprise, their trunks disappearing into a black hole below the trays.

At the far end of the garden, the silver workshop wall acts as a backdrop to the trays, and fiery red-hot pokers provide colorful accents. A white bench outside the workshop is both sculptural and functional.

▲ FLOATING PLATEAUS

ABOVE (TWO PICTURES) Tall, spiky architectural plants, such as cordylines, add a dynamic quality to the trays' smooth horizontal surfaces. Seen from this angle, the grass-topped trays look like three floating plateaus.

► BUBBLING UP

RIGHT (TWO PICTURES) The shiny, bubble-effect aluminum tiles used to clad the walls of the wooden workshop were hand-turned. Reflecting the garden in miniature, they also bounce light back into the garden.

Bordered on three sides by the trays, a pool is made safe for children and unsuspecting adults with a metal grille.

From the first moment I set foot in this garden, I knew the whole experience was going to be fun. The brief from the clients was clear, and although they wanted an Art Nouveau style I didn't particularly like, I was determined to create a garden that would be functional yet dramatic— despite the difficult sloping site. The garden already had two usable terraces linked by a set of steep steps, which I incorporated into my final design. The result is a dramatic social space using color, architecture, and plants to form a symmetrical celebration.

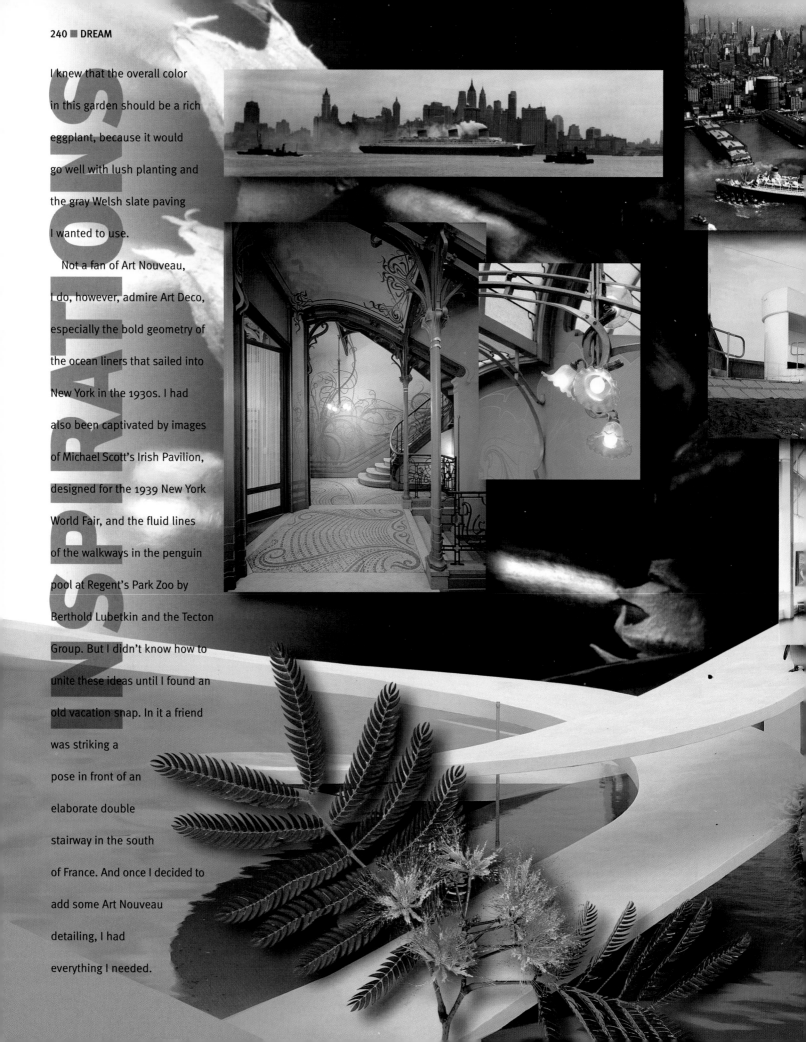

INSPIRATIONS

I knew that the overall color in this garden should be a rich eggplant, because it would go well with lush planting and the gray Welsh slate paving I wanted to use.

Not a fan of Art Nouveau, I do, however, admire Art Deco, especially the bold geometry of the ocean liners that sailed into New York in the 1930s. I had also been captivated by images of Michael Scott's Irish Pavilion, designed for the 1939 New York World Fair, and the fluid lines of the walkways in the penguin pool at Regent's Park Zoo by Berthold Lubetkin and the Tecton Group. But I didn't know how to unite these ideas until I found an old vacation snap. In it a friend was striking a pose in front of an elaborate double stairway in the south of France. And once I decided to add some Art Nouveau detailing, I had everything I needed.

At the top of the garden I designed an Italianate balcony flanked by a sweeping double staircase. I sketched an opening, with an Art Nouveau–style gate, between the stairs. This led to an existing shed, which I planned to retain for storage. At the bottom of the steps I designed a neat rectangular lawn, bordered by beds of verdant planting.

Access from here to the terrace closest to the house—which the clients wanted to use as a dining area—would be via a central staircase. The stairs on my plan dissected curved beds, built on three levels. These were designed to give the impression of cascades, with flowers and foliage flowing down the hill.

The structures in the garden were to be built from rendered concrete block and painted a luxurious eggplant, while the paving and steps would be slate. Wrought-iron railings and gates, designed in the elaborate and swirling Art Nouveau style, introduced the look that the clients wanted.

▼ SKETCHING IDEAS
It seemed to me that the best way to tackle the steep slope in this garden was to terrace it, using bold Art Deco structures and Art Nouveau details.

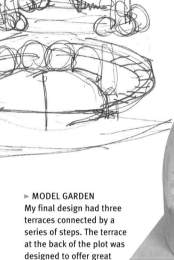

► MODEL GARDEN
My final design had three terraces connected by a series of steps. The terrace at the back of the plot was designed to offer great views of the garden.

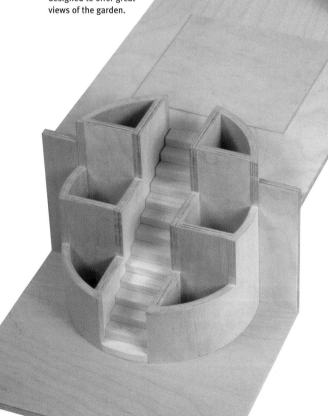

▼ FINISHED DESIGN
The hard landscaping was painted a rich eggplant color, which looks fantastic against the white hydrangea flowers.

The color green is hugely important in this garden because, as a calming shade, it links all the other colors and materials together.

The clients like traditional plants, and I wanted the planting to be as flamboyant as the garden's hard landscaping. For these reasons, I planted the wonderful *Hydrangea paniculata* 'Grandiflora' amid a sea of golden hostas. I also used aralias—large shrubs or small trees with spiny stems, dramatic foliage, and panicles of greenish white flowers.

Clouds of romantic cottage-garden-style planting fill the beds around the carpet of lawn. The plants here include: agapanthus, with their huge globes of trumpet-shaped flowers, followed by decorative seed heads; nerines, which have lilylike flowers in autumn; scented sage (*Salvia officinalis*); fragrant roses; and long-flowering verbenas.

PLANTS

PLANTING LIST

CLOCKWISE FROM TOP LEFT

Salvia officinalis
Golden hosta
Verbena bonariensis
Rosmarinus officinalis
Tulbaghia violacea
Catalpa bignonioides
Hydrangea paniculata 'Grandiflora'

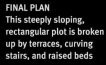

FINAL PLAN
This steeply sloping, rectangular plot is broken up by terraces, curving stairs, and raised beds

THE LOOKOUT
The balcony offers a bird's-eye view of the plants and flowers below

CURVED STAIRS
Two flights of stairs lead to the balcony, almost creating a circle

SHEER LAWN
The middle terrace has a small lawn that is quite easy to maintain

TIERED PLANTING
Three raised beds set within a circle are filled with colorful plants

PATIO TERRACE
The lower slate terrace provides space for dining and entertaining

This garden is an over-the-top celebration of fun. It's a theatrical fantasy, multilayered like a wedding cake—it should have two plastic statues of the bride and groom at the top! Marilyn Monroe would have been at home here, and I can see Fred Astaire and Ginger Rogers dancing down the double staircase.

The elaborate Art Nouveau style is captured in the details, especially the wrought-iron work, but the structures themselves are very simple. I've used a limited number of materials, which means that the plants don't have to compete with the structure for prominence.

Although this is a dramatic, quite overpowering garden, I like its boldness. People have criticized the scale of the structures, which I've crammed into quite a small space, but when you stand on the top terrace, you can see over the house and for miles around, and from this viewpoint the garden itself looks perfectly in proportion.

▲ SOFTENING THE EDGES

TOP MAIN PICTURE The heavy-looking structures are a counterpoise to the delicate Art Nouveau details, and create an exciting contrast. Behind the gate under the stairs, I positioned a mirror to act as a backdrop and to disguise the shed behind it.

To set off the rich, dark eggplant paintwork, I have used flamboyant white hydrangeas, trained into standards, shooting out of yellow hostas like frothy fountains.

▲ DEEP PURPLE

ABOVE (THREE PICTURES) The steps have a stagelike quality. Visitors are thrown into the spotlight as they descend, like movie stars of the 1920s and 1930s sweeping down ornate flights of stairs, making a spectacular entrance.

To add to the dramatic effect, I have flanked the elegant staircases with pencil-thin cypress trees planted in tall, white containers.

A rectangular lawn lies between the upper and lower terraces. This cool green space is designed for sunbathing and as relief from the hard structures and rich colors that surround it.

It's also interesting to watch how the sun changes the colors and forms in the garden. On cloudy days, the color of the eggplant structures is at full strength, but when the sun comes out it's knocked back to pale gray. This is why, in photographs taken on different days or from different angles, the structures can look a variety of colors.

▶ COLORS IN CLOSE-UP

OPPOSITE PAGE The lowest terrace, close to the house, is designed as an outdoor space for dining and entertaining, and set with a wooden table and chairs.

Sheltered by the house and the raised flower beds, this area has a feeling of warmth and enclosure. It also offers a dramatic view up the stairs to the top of the garden, leading the eye away from the boundaries and lifting it to the sky.

The publisher would like to thank the following for their kind permission to reproduce their photographs. Abbreviations key: t=top, b=below, r=right, l=left, c=center, f=far, a=above.

2 Image taken from page 212
4-5 Images taken from chapters later in the book; see details below
6 t © BBC Worldwide 2003/Robin Matthews; ac Diarmuid Gavin; bc The Irish Image Collection; b Joe Cornish/DK
7 t, c & b D. Gavin; ac D. Gavin (Dublin Botanic Garden); bc Colin Walton/DK
8 t & c D. Gavin (Royal Dublin Society Festival); b D. Gavin
9 tl D. Gavin (Garden Festival, Royal Hospital Kilmainham, Dublin, 1996); tr John Glover (Gavin Landscapes, Chelsea Flower Show, 1995); c, bl & bc D. Gavin; cr Gary Rogers/RHS Press Office (Chelsea Flower Show, 1996); br © BBC Worldwide 2003/Robin Matthews

10 PHILOSOPHIES

10-11 t & b Neil Gavin; ac C. Walton; c Brian North
12 Clive Boursnell. Courtesy of Headline Publishing *The Curious Gardeners Six Elements of Garden Design*
13 tl Clive Boursnell/Garden Picture Library; tc John Sleeman/Tony Heywood Conceptual Gardens ('Split', Westonbirt International Festival of Gardens, 2003); tr John Ferro Sims/GPL (Lady Walton, La Mortella, Ischia. Design: Russell Page); cl Helen Dillon; c Gill Shaw/RHS Press Office; cr Concrete Information Ltd (Frank Newberry); bl Transworld Publishing/Bluebridge Studios, Halstead; bc & br Steven Wooster/GPL
14 t Elizabeth Whiting & Associates/Alamy; c V&A Picture Library (Design: Robin Day); b Chris Moore (Design: Philip Treacy)
15 t Andrew Southall/arcblue.com (Architect: Future Systems); b Bill Bachmann/Alamy
16 t C. Nichols (Chelsea Flower Show, 1997. Design: Christopher Bradley-Hole); b C. Nichols (Chelsea Flower Show, 2002. Design: Stephen Woodhams)
17 www.the-hempel.co.uk
18 Suzie Gibbons/GPL (Chelsea Flower Show, 2002. Design: Mary Reynolds)
19 t Andrew Lawson Photography/Alamy; b Robert Harding Picture Library/Alamy
20 t Arcaid/Alamy; b J. Buckley
21 tl & cl Gay Bumgarner/Alamy; tc & tr GPL/Alamy; c Stock Connection Inc/Alamy; cr DK; bl Rubberball/Alamy; bc E.J. Baumeister Jr/Alamy; br plainpicture/Alamy

22 t B. North; b DK
23 t Wayne Hutchinson/Holt Studios; c plainpictures/Alamy; b GPL/Alamy
24 J. Glover/DK
25 t Mark Bolton/GPL; c DK; b Christopher Fairweather/GPL
26 t C. Nichols; b DK
27 tl Neil Holmes/GPL; tc Carol Sharp/Flowerphotos; tr J.S. Sira/GPL; cl M. Bolton/GPL; c & cr DK; bl Neil Fletcher/DK; bc & br J. Buckley/DK
28 Alex Bartel/Arcaid
29 t Richard Davies (Architect: Future Systems); c David Crausby/Alamy; b Tim Street-Porter (Architect: Luis Barragan)
30 t Paul Raftery/View (Architect: Le Corbusier); c From the Collections of Henry Ford Museum & Greenfield Village (Design: Richard Buckminster Fuller); b Richard Einzig/Arcaid (Architect: Richard Rogers)
31 David Silverman/Travel Ink

32 THE GARDENS

32-33 © BBC Worldwide 2003/Robin Matthews

34 UNWIND

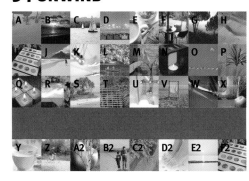

34-35 A, B, E, H, O, W: © C. Walton; C, K, N, Q, U, Z: C. Walton/DK; D: Shaen Adey/DK; F, I, M, P, R, T, X, A2, C2, F2: J. Buckley; L, S, V: Rob Reichenfeld/DK; Y: Ian O'Leary/DK; B2: J. Cornish/DK; D2: Ruth Jenkinson/DK

36 CUBE

36-37 J. Buckley

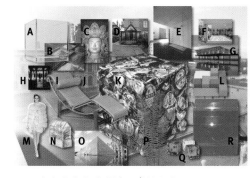

38-39 A, L, P, Q, R: C. Walton/DK; B: Beren Patterson/Alamy; C: Sami Sarkis/Alamy;

D: www.conservatoriesbywestbury.com; E: Original Bathrooms Ltd; F: Jerry Harpur (Design: Raymond Hudson, Bloomberg, South Africa); G: Southport pier pavilion (Architect: Shed KM) Chris Brink/View; H: Cloisters of Iford Manor, Wilts. Heather Angel/Natural Visions; I: Le Corbusier lounger/DK; J: The Louvre, Paris. Setboun/Corbis; K: Advertising Archive; M: Celine's Autumn/Winter 2003-04 ready-to-wear collection (Design: Michael Kors) Xavier Lhospice/Reuters 2003; N: RBG Kew; O: Glass Pyramid, The Louvre, Paris (Architect: I.M. Pei) Robert Harding Picture Library/Alamy
40 t D. Gavin; b J. Buckley
41 tl A. Lawson/DK; tr, cr & bcl DK; cl Picturesmiths/DK; bcr Marcus Harpur; b M. Bolton/GPL
42-43 J. Buckley

44 GREENHOUSE

44-45 J. Buckley

46-47 A: Corrugated iron tunneler's cottage, Arthur's Pass village, New Zealand; Lloyd Park/DK; B: Gateshead Millennium Bridge (Architects: Wilkinson Eyre) www.graeme-peacock.com; C, D: DK; E: Chateau de Corbeil, Cerf, France (Design: Pascal Cribier) J. Harpur; F: Botermelk, Nr Antwerp (Design: Jacques Wirtz) Patrick Taylor; G: Shepherd House, Inveresk. J. Harpur; H: Matthew Ward/DK; I: C. Walton/DK; J: www.eden-greenhouses.co.uk; K: Eden, Cornwall. Peter Anderson; L: Dublin Botanic Gardens. C. Walton/DK; M: Cadillace Coupe de Ville. Dave King/DK; N: The New Beetle, 2003 www.volkswagen.co.uk
48 J. Buckley
49 tl, tr & b DK; cl David England/GPL; cr C. Fairweather/GPL; bcl J. Harpur; bcr James Young/DK
50-51 J. Buckley

52 CONCRETE

52-53 J. Buckley
54-55 A: Miyagi Stadium Sendai, Japan (Architect: atelier Hitoshi Abe) Dennis Gilbert/View; B: Hilliers Nurseries; C: www.civictrees.co.uk; D: Private garden, Bloomberg, South Africa (Design: Raymond Hudson) J. Harpur; E: Isokon building, North London (Architect: Wells Coates) Jefferson smith/arcblue.com; F: Private

garden, New Zealand (Design: Ted Smyth) Gil Hanly; G: BBC Demonstration Gardens, Birmingham (Design: Bonita Bulaitis) Andrea Jones/Garden Exposures Photo Library; H: Royal Festival Hall, London (Architects: Robert Matthews & Leslie Martin) Peter Durant/arcblue.com; I: Stadelhofen station, Zurich (Architect: Santiago Calatrava) Alberto Piovano/Arcaid; J: Langham Lakes, Dorset. Andrea Jones/Garden Exposures Photo Library; K: www.moderngarden.co.uk; L: South Bank complex (Architect: Denys Casdun) Grant Smith/View; M: C. Walton/DK; N: Stockwell Bus Garage. RIBA Library Photographs Collection

56 J. Buckley
57 tl Beth Chatto/DK; tr, cr, bcl & bcr DK; cl Juliette Wade/DK; b B. Thomas/GPL
58 l, tr & br J. Buckley; cr C. Nichols
59 l & c J. Buckley; r C. Nichols

60 NATURE

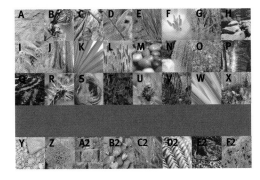

60-61 A, C, S, D2: C. Walton/DK; D, F, H, K, M, N, O, Q, R, U, W, Z, A2, C2, E2: © C. Walton; B: Jerry Young/DK; E: Deni Bown/DK; G, V, X: © BBC Worldwide 2003/Robin Matthews; I, P, Y: DK; J: Candace Kenyon/Ministry of Forests, British Columbia; L: David Burton; T: Anne Hyde/DK; B2: Howard Rice/DK; F2: Jacqui Hurst/DK

62 SYLVAN

62-63 © BBC Worldwide 2003/Robin Matthews
64-65 A: Nigel Curtiss's apartment Ocean 6, Tokyo. Deidi von Schaewen; B: G. Rogers/GPL; C: DK; D: Marrakesh, Morocco. Ken Hayden/Red Cover; E: Casa Mila, Barcelona (Architect: Antonio Gaudi) Andrew Holt/View; F: Yarrawa Hill, Southern Highlands, NSW,

Australia (Architect: Mark Jones) Richard Glover/View; G: Florida, USA. Fraser Hall/Robert Harding Picture Library; H: C. Walton/DK; I: Chris Tubbs/Red Cover; J: Sears Tower, Chicago. Andrew Leyerie/DK; K: Dundalk Freight Depot, Co. Louth by David Hughes, Iarnrod Eireann Architects. Carmel McCormack/Gandon Archive, Kinsale; L: N. Fletcher/DK; M: Boating pavilion, River Thames, Berkshire (Architects: Brookes Stacey Randall & Bree Day) Peter Durant/arcblue.com; N: U-Bein Bridge, Myanmar. Norma Joseph/Robert Harding Picture Library

66 t D. Gavin; b BBC Worldwide 2003/Robin Matthews
67 tl A. Lawson; tr, cl, cr, bcr & b DK; bcl H. Rice/DK
68-69 © BBC Worldwide 2003/Robin Matthews

70 CURVY

70-71 © BBC Worldwide 2003/Robin Matthews

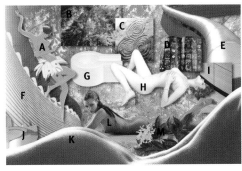

72-73 A: Illustrative plate of Josephine Baker dancing wearing banana skirt by Paul Colin from Le Tumulte Noir. V&A Picture Library; B (and background): Naturepl.com; C: Triple spiral, New Grange, Co. Meath, Ireland. Michael Jenner/Robert Harding Picture Library; D: Derry Watkins. www.specialplants.net; E: C. Walton; F: Expo site, Seville. C. Walton; G, I, M: C. Walton/DK; H: Advertising Archive; J: Vitra Museum, Germany (Architect: Frank Gehry) Philip Kierle/Architectural Association; K: Powerstock; L: Freundin/Robert Harding Picture Library
74 © BBC Worldwide 2003/Robin Matthews
75 tl DK; tr David Cavagnaro/GPL; cl J.S. Sira/GPL; cr C. Nichols/GPL; bcl J. Harpur; bcr M. Bolton/GPL; b J. Glover/GPL
76-77 © BBC Worldwide 2003/Robin Matthews

78 BOAT

78-79 © BBC Worldwide 2003/Robin Matthews

80-81 A: Architect: David Shepherd, Devon; B, E, F, H, K: Norfolk Broads. David Burton; C: DK; D: Jon Spaull/DK; G: Bogland, Ireland. D. Gavin; I: 'Holding Pattern' A permanent light work on the A13, East London by Tom de Paor, Graham Ellard & Stephen Johnstone. Paul Bookless; J: (Architect: Herb Greene) Tim Street-Porter
82 © BBC Worldwide 2003/Robin Matthews
83 tl & tr DK; cl James Young/DK; cr, bcl & b Picturesmiths/DK; bcr Didier Willery/GPL
84-85 © BBC Worldwide 2003/Robin Matthews

86 PLAY

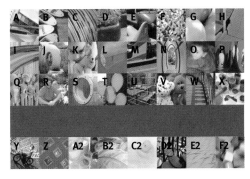

86-87 A: DK; B, E, F, H, K, M, O, Q, T, W, B2: C. Walton; C, I, J, Z: © BBC Worldwide 2003/Robin Matthews; D, L, N, S, U: J. Buckley; G, V, X, A2, C2, E2, F2: C. Walton/DK; P: Maurice Agis's Dreamspace/P. Broton; R: John Colley; Y: Getty Images

88 WIRED

88-89 J. Buckley

90-91 A: © Desperate Dan/D C Thomson & Co. Ltd;

B: Temperate rainforest, New England National Park, Australia. Heather Angel/Natural Visions; C: *Dicksonia fibrosa*. Geoff Moon/Natural Visions; D: Post Ranch Inn, Big Sur, California (Architect: Mickey Muenning) Alan Weintraub/Arcaid; E: The Snowdon Aviary, London Zoo. The Zoological Society of London; F, I: DK; G: Peckham Library, London (Architect: Alsop & Stormer) Richard Glover/View; H: Sydney aquarium. Alan Williams/DK; J: Public park. Los Angeles. Arthur Coddington/Alamy; K: 'Away From the Flock' Damien Hirst. Courtesy of The Saatchi Gallery, London

92 J. Buckley

93 tl, cl & cr DK; tr C. Nichols; bcl J. Harpur; bcr H. Rice/GPL; b J. Wade/DK

94-95 J. Buckley

96 FLORA'S GARDEN

96-97 © BBCWorldwide 2003/Robin Matthews

98-99 A: Brock Elbank/Red represents; B: Design: Jessica Duncan. Marianne Majerus; C: Crete. Max Alexander/DK; D: Pelargoniums. Jon Bouchier/GPL; E: Flora; F: Cerdigion, Wales (Architect: Alexander Potter) Alex Ramsay/Red Cover; G: Mykonos, Greece. Linda Whitman/DK; H: C. Walton/DK; I: Chris Ofili's home. East London (Architects: Adjaye & Russell) R. Davies

100 D. Gavin

101 tl H. Rice/GPL; tr, cr & bcr DK; cl J. Glover/GPL; bcl C. Nichols/GPL; b Andrew Butler/DK

102-103 © BBC Worldwide 2003/Robin Matthews

104 SLINKY

104-105 © BBC Worldwide 2003/Robin Matthews

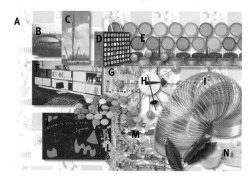

106-107 A: (background) 'Flowerpots' furnishing fabric designed by Tom Mellors and made by D.

Whitehead Ltd. Daniel McGrath/V&A Picture Library; B: Festival of Britain exhibition ground 1951. Hulton Deutsch Collection/Corbis; C: 300ft Skylon, Festival of Britain 1951. Hulton Deutsch Collection/Corbis; D & N: C. Walton/DK; E: George Nelson's Marshmallow sofa. Hans Hansen/www.vitra.com; F: Utility storage units designed by R. Day for Heal & Sons. Heal's Archive/V&A Picture Library; G: 'Rig' textile designed by Lucien Day. V&A Picture Library; H: Copper-Hewitt, National Design Museum, Smithsonian Institute: Gift of Mel Byars; I: Slinky. C. Walton/DK; J: Joan Miro's 'A Star Caresses the Breast of a Negress' oil on canvas 1938. Tate Picture Library; K: Smarties. C. Walton/DK; L: *Prunus lusitanica*. Matthew Ward/DK; M: Furnishing fabric by Cuno Rischer. V&A Picture Library

108 t D. Gavin; b BBC Worldwide 2003/Robin Matthews

109 tl Derek St Romaine; tr H. Rice/DK; cl Picturesmiths/DK; cr H. Rice/GPL; bcl DK; bcr N. Holmes/GPL; b J. Harpur

110-111 ©BBC Worldwide 2003/Robin Matthews except; bl John Colley

112 EGGHEAD

112-113 © BBC Worldwide 2003/Robin Matthews

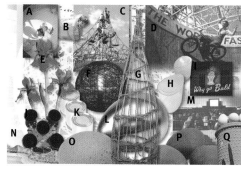

114-115 A: Getty Images; D: Wall of Death, Southend. Hulton Archive; B: Early Learning Centre; C: Ecoscene/PT; E: DK; F: 'Customs House Memorial' by sculptor Yann Renard Goulet, Dublin. The Irish Image Collection; G: Steve Gorton/DK; H, I, K, L, O, P: C. Walton/DK; J: David Burton; N: Parc Guell, Barcelona (Architect: A. Gaudi) Erika Craddock/GPL; Q: Salvador Dali Museum, Figueres, Spain. C. Bowman/Robert Harding Picture Library

116 © BBC Worldwide 2003/Robin Matthews

117 tl DK; tr H. Rice/DK; cl J. Glover/DK; cr Deni Bown/DK; bcl J.S. Sira/GPL; bcr & b Picturesmiths/DK

118-119 © BBC Worldwide 2003/Robin Matthews

120 POD

120-121 J. Buckley

122-123 A: www.dreamspace-agis.com. P. Brotons; B: Tree house. L'Ecole Des Beaux Arts D'Angers, Chaumont Festival, 2002. J. Harpur; C: Lugris/Alamy; D: C. Walton; E: New National Gallery, Berlin (Architect: Mies van der Rohe) Sarah Farmer/Architectural Association; F: Design: Shaun

Leane. Eitan Lee; G: 'A Grand Day Out'. © NFTS 1989; H: Artwork by D. Gavin; I: Dreamspace 2000 by Maurice Agis. D. Launder; J, M: C. Walton/DK; K: Hotel Arts with Fish, Barcelona. F. Gehry. Clara Kraft/Architectural Association; L: White plastic boomerang desk designed by Maurice Calka, for Leleu-Deshay, 1969. France. Christies Images 2003

124 t D. Gavin; b J. Buckley

125 tl & b DK; tr J. Harpur; cl S. Wooster/DK; cr H. Rice/GPL

126-127 J. Buckley

128 INSPIRE

128-129 A: DK; J, L, M, O, P, Q, R, T, V, F2: C. Walton; C, D, F, H, I, N, S, Y, A2, D2, E2: C. Walton/DK; B: H. Rice/DK; E, W, Z: J. Buckley; G: Deni Bown/DK; K: Peter Cook/View; U, X, C2: © BBC Worldwide 2003/Robin Matthews; B2: David Murray/DK

130 ARTHOUSE

130-131 J. Buckley

132-133 A: (background) C. Walton/DK; B: 'Lakeside Studio', Sacramento (Architect: Mark Dziewulski) www.dzarchitect.com; C: Everglades, Florida. Hoa-

Qui/Robert Harding Picture Library; D: Bali (Design: Linda Garland) J. Harpur; E: Co. Galway. Sylvain Grandadam/Robert Harding Picture Library; F: Alaska Stock/Robert Harding Picture Library; G, K: Maldives. www.itcclassics.co.uk; H: 'Night Portrait' 1978, Lucien Freud. Bridgeman Art Library; I, L: Everglades, Florida. David Burton; J: Zachary House, Louisiana. Tim Hursley; M: The Grove, Oxon. The late David Hicks. Peter Baistow/GPL; N: *Nymphaea carnea*. Derek St Romaine; O: Florida swamp. Dave King/DK; P: Powerstock; Q: www.factoryfurniture.co.uk

134 t D. Gavin; b J. Buckley

135 tl & cr DK; tr A. Lawson/DK; cl J. Buckley /DK; b J.S. Sira/GPL

136-137 J. Buckley

138 SPHERE

138-139 © BBC Worldwide 2003/Robin Matthews

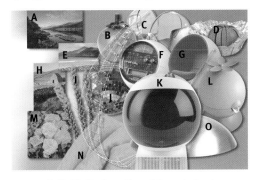

140-141 A, H: Moll's Gap, Ring of Kerry, Ireland. J. Cornish/DK; B, D, F, J, L, N, O: C. Walton/DK; C, G: Chairs designed by Eero Aarnio. www.adelta.de & www.eero-aarnio.com; E: Glen Veigh, Co. Kerry, Ireland. D. Gavin; I: Liatris spicata. C. Walton/DK; K: Videosphere. Courtesy of Simon Alderson, Twentieth Century Design; M: *Rosa* 'Wiltshire'. H. Rice/DK

142 t D. Gavin; b © BBC Worldwide 2003/Robin Matthews

143 tl, cl & cr DK; tr A. Lawson/DK; bcl & bcr J. Glover/GPL; b J. Harpur

144-145 © BBC Worldwide 2003/Robin Matthews

146 THE OVAL

146-147 © BBC Worldwide 2003/Robin Matthews

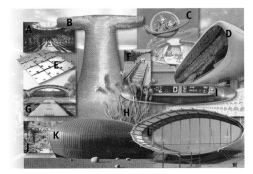

148-149 A: 'Close Encounters of a Third Kind'. The Kobal Collection; B: Some/One, 2001. Courtesy of

Do-Ho Suh and Lehmann Maupin Gallery, New York and Serpentine Gallery press Office; C: The Jetsons. Capital Pictures; D: Lords Media Centre, London (Architect: Future Systems) Peter Cook/View; E: C. Walton/DK; F: Photo by Chris Hodson, supplied by the 'Copper in Architecture' campaign. www.cda.org.uk/arch; G: Bus shelter, Dundalk, Co. Louth by David Hughes & Irene Coveney, Iarnod Eireann Architects, 1995. Carmel McCormack/Gandon Archive, Kinsale; H: Lavandula stoechas. C. Walton/DK; I: www.citroen.co.uk; J: Design: Thomas Church. J. Harpur; K: Dutch National Heritage Museum, Mecanoo Architects. Paul Raftery/View; L: Cardiff Bay Visitors Centre (Architects: Alsop & Stormer) Mike Jones/Architectual Association

150 t D. Gavin; br © BBC Worldwide 2003/Robin Matthews; bl (both) Elma Murray

151 tl A. Lawson/DK; tr & bcl DK; cl J. Buckley /DK; cr Juliette Wade/DK; bcr Eric Crichton/DK; b Deni Bown/DK

152-153 © BBC Worldwide 2003/Robin Matthews

154 STEEL TUNNELS

154-155 J. Buckley

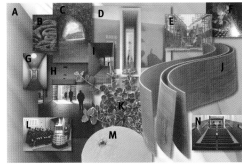

156-157 A: (background) Irish flag. C. Walton/DK; B: Maze at Glendurgan, Cornwall. Robert Harding Picture Library/Alamy; C: DK; D: 'Red Wall', Moutard Design. Richard Waite; E: AKG London; F: Robert Harding Picture Library/Alamy; G: Alan Schein Photography/Corbis; H, I , M, N: C. Walton/DK; J: 'Snake' 1994-1996 Richard Serra. Guggenheim, Bilbao. Bridgeman Art Library; K: Euonymus. C. Walton/DK; L: 'Daleks - Invasion Earth 2150 AD', Doctor Who, 1966 AARU Prods/The Kobal Collection

158 t D. Gavin; b J. Buckley

159 tl, tr, bcl & bcr DK; cl S. Wooster/DK; bcr C. Walton/DK; b M. Harpur

160-161 J. Buckley

162 PARTY

162-163 A, B, C, D, E, H, K, M, N, P, Q, R, U, Y, Z, B2, C2, D2, F2: C. Walton/DK; F, I, O, S, X, A2: C. Walton; G, J, T, V, E2: © BBC Worldwide 2003/Robin Matthews; L: Dave King/DK; W: John Bulmer/DK

164 TRAIN

164-165© BBC Worldwide 2003/Robin Matthews

166-167 A, I: Manchester airport. Ian Howarth; B: 'Antiques from the Garden' by Alistair Morris; C: San Francisco cable car. Simon Harris/Robert Harding Picture Library; D: Fotoccompli; E: Image Source Ltd/Alamy; F: Gavin Watson/PYMCA; G: 'Composition with Red, Yellow and Blue' 1930 Piet Mondrian. Bridgeman Art Library; H: Fountains at Somerset House, London (Architects: Dixon Jones/William Chambers). Dennis Gilbert/View; J: Courtesy of Jamiroquai Ltd/Video director: Jonathan Glazer, Sony Music; K: Light boxes by Calumet/www.calumetphoto.com; L: BBC, Top of the Pops; M: www.shopkit.com; N: Heidi Weber Haus, Zurich (Architect: Le Corbusier) Walter Rawlings/Robert Harding Picture Library; O: Gateway Orientation Centre, Loch Lomond, Scotland (Architect: Bennetts Associates) Keith Hunter/arcblue.com; P: Villa Savoye, Poissy, France (Architect: Le Corbusier) Paul Raftery/View; Q: Euphorbia. DK; R: www.railimages.co.uk; S: Philip Johnson residence and pavilion, New Caanan, Connecticut, 1963. Julius Shulman; T: C. Walton; U: Japanese Bullet train. Jim Winkley/Ecoscene

168 © BBC Worldwide 2003/Robin Matthews

169 tl Deni Bown/DK; tr Derek St Romaine; cl Ron Sutherland/GPL; cr Jerry Pavia/GPL; bcl Justyn Willsmore; bcr J. Harpur; b M. Harpur

170-171 © BBC Worldwide 2003/Robin Matthews

172 CAVES

172-173 © BBC Worldwide 2003/Robin Matthews

174-175 A: International Stock/Robert Harding Picture Library; B: (background) Orange arena, France. C. Walton; C: Soft and Hairy house, Japan (Architect: Ushida Findlay) Katsuhisa Kida; D: Cave Dwellings, Cappadocia, Turkey. Jonathan Blair/Corbis; E: Futuristic residence, South France (Architect: Antti Lovag); F: *Cotinus* 'Grace' DK; G: The GUINNESS word the HARP device and ARTHUR GUINNESS signature are trade marks and are reproduced together with the Igloo advertisement (Faiyaz Jafri www.unit.nl and Jeremy Carr, agency: AMV BBDO) with kind permission of Guinness & Co. All rights reserved; H: Caves, Turkey. DK; I: Truss Wall House, Japan (Architect: Ushida Findlay) Kenji Shimizu; J: Spraying concrete onto 'Twin Cone'. A13 Artscape project for London Borough of Barking and Dagenham; K: Truss Wall House, Japan (Architect: Ushida Findlay) Katsuhisa Kida; L: Private house, Surrey (Architect: John Newton) John Edward Linden/Arcaid

176 t D. Gavin; b © BBC Worldwide 2003/Robin Matthews

177 tl & b A. Lawson; tr Brian Carter/GPL; cl & bcl C. Nichols; cr C. Nichols/GPL; bcr J. Harpur

178-189 © BBC Worldwide 2003/Robin Matthews

180 HOVERCRAFT

180-181 © BBC Worldwide 2003/Robin Matthews

182-183 A: Brand X Pictures/Alamy; B: San Francisco bay. Jack Fields/Corbis; C: © Yachting World/IPC Syndication; D: Ion accelerator and Volt generator. Powerstock; E: David Burton; F: Crocosmia. C. Walton/DK; G: South Beach, Florida. Gavin Hellier/Robert Harding Picture Library; H: State

Capitol Bank, Oklahoma City, 1963 (Architects: Bailey, Bozalis, Dickinson, Roloff) Julius Shulman

184 t D. Gavin; b © BBC Worldwide 2003, Robin Matthews

185 tl S. Wooster/DK; tr, cl & cr DK; bcl Juliette Wade/DK; bcr J. Glover/GPL; b Ron Evans/GPL

186-187 © BBC Worldwide 2003/Robin Matthews

188 BOX

188-189 © BBC Worldwide 2003/Robin Matthews

190-191 A: Japanese interior. Arcaid/Alamy; B, O: C. Walton/DK; C: Powerstock; D: Wimbledon. Michael Jenner/Robert Harding Picture Library; E: Storm Stanley/Robert Harding Picture Library; F: Adam Woolfitt/Robert Harding Picture Library; G, L: Houghton's Horses Picture Library; H: Oxford Scientific Films; I: Treehouse (Design: Jeff Bale, Portland) J. Harpur; J: Hong Kong container terminal. Tim Hal/Robert Harding Picture Library; K: Philip Johnson residence and pavilion, New Caanan, Connecticut. Julius Shulman; M: *Clematis* 'Arabella' Derek St Romaine; N: Container City, London (Architect: Nicholas Lacey) Richard Booth/Architectural Association; P: David Burton

192 © BBC Worldwide 2003/Robin Matthews

193 tl, tr, cl & bcr DK; cr Bob Rundle/DK; bcl Joseph Strauch/DK; b H. Rice/ GPL

194-195 © BBC Worldwide 2003/Robin Matthews

196 DREAM

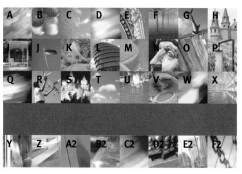

196-197 A, B, C, E, F, J, L, N, O, S, U, W, Y, F2: C. Walton; D, Q, A2, C2: C. Walton/DK; G: Nigel Francis/Robert Harding Picture Library; H, T: DK; I, M, B2, E2: © BBC Worldwide 2003/Robin Matthews; K, P, V, D2: J. Buckley; R: Powerstock; X: Greg Delves;

Z: Peter Cook/View

198 SHARK'S FIN

198-199 J. Buckley

200-201 A: Powerstock; B: Bradford, Yorkshire. Adam Woolfitt/Robert Harding Picture Library; C: www.anglering.co.uk; D: *Cordyline australis*. Heather Angel/Natural Visions; E, L, M: DK; F: Tree ferns. Ayrlies, Auckland, NZ. Beverley McConnell. J. Harpur; G: Iron gate. Charney Well. Cumbria. Marianne Majerus; H: Well of Wisdom Japanese Garden, Tully, Ireland. Heather Angel/Natural Visions; I: Sculpture. Liverpool Street station. C. Walton; J: Agapanthus. J. Buckley/DK; K: Ron Sutherland/GPL; N: Headington, Oxford. Nigel Francis/Robert Harding Picture Library; O: The Orkney Stone Company; P: Peter Durant/arcblue.com

202 t D. Gavin; b J. Buckley

203 tl, tr & cr DK; cl J. Buckley /DK; bcl H. Rice/GPL; bcr Floribunda/GPL; b N. Holmes/DK

204-205 J. Buckley

206 AIRPLANE

206-207 © BBC Worldwide 2003/Robin Matthews

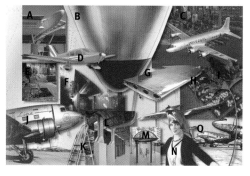

208-209 A: Charles de Gaulle Airport (Architect: Paul Andreu Aeroports de Paris) Andrew Southall/arcblue.com; B: Frank Schramm; C, J, N: Powerstock; D: Richard Leeney/DK; E: Abello, Madrid. Design: Arabella Lennox-Boyd. J. Harpur; F: Architects: Adrian Koerfer & Jurgen Willen. D. Leistner/artur; www.avionart.com; H: C. Walton/DK; I: *Heuchera* 'Chocolate Veil'. Derek St Romaine; K: Matthew Ward/DK; L: Cannon Avent office, Suffolk (Architect: Fletcher Priest) Chris Gascoigne/View; M: Neil Lukas/DK; O: Douglas

planes. Museum of Flight/Corbis
210 © BBC Worldwide 2003/Robin Matthews
211 tl Gil Hanly; tr H. Rice/GPL; cl C. Nichols/GPL;
cr Emma Peios/GPL; b Justyn Willsmore
212-213 © BBC Worldwide 2003/Robin Matthews

214 HOLLYWOOD

214-215 © BBC Worldwide 2003/Robin Matthews

216-217 A, D, I, N: C. Walton/DK; B: U2 concert. Roisin
McMurray/Redferns; C: 'Golddiggers of 1933', Busby
Berkeley. Courtesy Warner Bros./Dalton Nicholson
Collection; E: www.limestonegallery.com; F:
Reproduced courtesy of Carlton International Media
Ltd./LFI; G: Joan Crawford. 1936. George Hurrell/The
Kobal Collection; H: City Hall, London (Architect: Sir
Norman Foster and Partners) C. Walton; J: Bob Hope
with Oscars at the Academy Awards/The Kobal
Collection; K: Michael Jenner/Robert Harding Picture
Library; L: *Fatsia japonica*. C. Walton/DK; M: Courtesy
of the Savoy/The American Bar
218 t D. Gavin; b © BBC Worldwide 2003/Robin
Matthews
219 tl DK; tr S. Wooster/DK; cl Justyn Willsmore;
cl & b John Fielding
220-221 © BBC Worldwide 2003/Robin Matthews

222 LAWN

222-223 J. Buckley

224-225 A (background) & G: Courtesy of Frances
Lincoln Publishers; B: Temple of Ancient Virtue,
Stowe Landscape Gardens. Nigel Francis/GPL;
C: Pensthorpe, Norfolk. Design: Piet Oudolf.
N. Holmes/GPL; D: Matmata, Tunisia. Dr. A.C.
Waltham/Robert Harding Picture Library; E: Swift's
Gulliver's Travels, Mary Evans Picture Library; F: Golf
course, The Mumbles, Wales. David Toase/Travel Ink;
H: Brand X Pictures/Alamy; I, L, P, Q: C. Walton/DK;
J: Southern Morocco. Mel Watson; K: 19th Century
Paisley design for shawl by George Charles Haite.
V&A Picture Library; M: www.limestonegallery.com;
N: 'The Matterhorn', Friar Park, Henley-on-Thames;
O: Nick Walker; R: *Miscanthus sinensis*.
C. Walton/DK; S: Bellagio, Las Vegas. C. Walton
226 t D. Gavin; b J. Buckley
227 tl & cr H. Rice/DK; tr & bcl DK; cl M. Bolton, GPL;
bcr A. Lawson; b C. Fairweather/GPL
228-229 J. Buckley

230 TRAY

230-231 J. Buckley

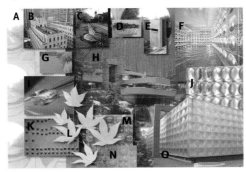

232-233 A: J. Buckley; B: Rockefeller Center, New
York. Nigel Francis, GPL; C: Kensington Roof Garden.
John Miller/GPL; D: www.oceanoutdoor.com;
E: Design: Paul Thompson & Trevyn McDowell.
C. Nichols/GPL; F: Swimming pool at Lennie Kravitz
home, Miami (Architect: Michael Czysz) Greg Delves;
G: Marianne Majerus; H: 'Falling Water' (Architect:
Frank Lloyd Wright). Peter Cook/View; I: Courtesy of
Max Power; J: C. Walton/DK; K: Door, Morocco. Mel
Watson; L: Acer leaves. Derek St Romaine; M, N:
www.hipprops.com; O: Elephant & Castle, London.
C. Walton/DK
234 t D. Gavin; b J. Buckley
235 tl C. Nichols; tr & b M. Harpur; cl H. Rice/DK;
cr S. Wooster/DK; bcl H. Rice/GPL; bcr Deni Bown/DK
236-237 J. Buckley

238 GARDEN NOUVEAU

238-239 © BBC Worldwide 2003/Robin Matthews

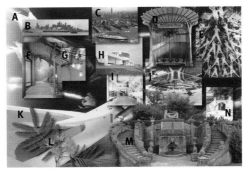

240-241 A: (background) Aubergines. C. Walton/DK;
B, C: New York. The Mariner's Museum/Corbis;
D: Porte Dauphine metro station (Architect: Hector
Guimard) Paul Raftery/View; E: 'Footlight Parade'
1933. Warner Bros./The Kobal Collection; F: Hotel
Tassel, Brussels. C. Bastin & J Evrard; G: Victor Horta
House Museum, Brussels. Richard Bryant/Arcaid;
H: Canvey Island, Essex (Architect: Ove Arup) Nick
Dawe/Arcaid; I: The Irish pavilion, New York World
Fair by Michael Scott Architect, 1939. Albert
Rothschild/Gandon Archive, Kinsale; J: Dublin airport
(Architect: Desmond Fitzgerald, Office of Public
Works, 1940) Gandon Archive, Kinsale; K: Penguin
pool, London Zoo (Architect; Berthold Lubetkin) Peter
Cook/View; L: Albizia julibrissin. Matthew Ward/DK;
M: Bowood House, Wiltshire. Nigel Francis/GPL;
N: D. Gavin
242 © BBC Worldwide 2003/Robin Matthews
243 tl C. Nichols; tr J. Buckley /DK; cl H. Rice/DK;
cr A. Lawson/DK; bcl Lamontagne/GPL; bcr John
Fielding (Blackthorn Nursery); b John Fielding;
244-245 © BBC Worldwide 2003/Robin Matthews

Endpapers: J. Buckley

the publishers thank...

THE IN-HOUSE TEAM
Senior Editor Zia Allaway
Senior Managing Editor Anna Kruger
Senior Managing Art Editor Lee Griffiths
Editors Vicky Willan, and Christine Dyer
DTP Designer Louise Waller
Picture Librarian Lucy Claxton
Production Controller Heather Hughes
Dorling Kindersley would also like to thank
Pamela Brown, Claire Bowers, and Kate Ledwith

Picture Research Melanie Watson
Photoshop Work (Inspirations pages) Richard Evans
Illustrations (Final garden plans) on pages 67, 75, 93, 135, 177, 185, and 203 Richard Lee
Garden Models Sean Cunningham

THIS BOOK WAS DESIGNED FOR DORLING KINDERSLEY BY WALTONCREATIVE.COM
Art Director Colin Walton
Art Editor Peter Radcliffe
Design Assistant Tracy Musson

Diarmuid thanks...

This collection is the result of a huge amount of work by many people. Thank you to everyone.

Especially Justine Keane—for sharing life with me. Sean Cunningham for garden and model-building, and friendship. Nik Linnen for guidance and patience, and Katherine, Polly, Petra, Brian, and Kati at John Noel Management.

Special thanks to Jane Root, Rachel Innes-Lumsden, Dan Adamson, Tom Archer, Laurence and Jackie Llewelyn-Bowen, Dave Smith, and David Symonds.

For fantastic photos: Robin Matthews, Jonathan Buckley, Neil Gavin (abrigado), and Elma Murray.

To Paul Cunningham for his continued presence.

Making this book was a fantastic experience. Thank you to David Lamb for understanding what I'm about.
To Zia Allaway for running it so well and appreciating the gardens so much.

To Colin Walton for his ideas, zeal, creativity, and wit.
To Mel Watson for unbelievable picture research—going beyond the call of duty.
To Richard Evans for the montages, and Peter Radcliffe for design.
To Lee Griffiths for quality control on design.
To Vicky Willan, Christine Dyer, and, of course, Anna Kruger, who all know their words.
To Louise Waller for all her technical help.

To Jack and Joan Gavin, Declan, Niamh, Emer, Susan, Gerry, David, Rebecca, Jack, Ella, and Hannah.
Terry and Ronan Keane, Madeline, Tim, Jane, Karl, Natasha, Julia, Holly, and Ben.
To the Byrnes in Billericay, the Mannings in Liverpool, Ann and Jay next door, Karen and Sally at Jaguar. Paul Martin and Steve Davis at AIB.
Ryan and Tom at Elite, Jay, Tony, Richard, Branton, Jason and Sam.

Jackie and Howard Tyson for their hospitality.
Denise and William, Warwick and Sally, Matthew and Kim, Angela and Dennis, Hayden and Mandy.